Dedication

I dedicate this book to my family,

To Grace, for being the magnificent, brave prince she is. Without her resilient confidence in my abilities, I'm not sure I would have been able to ward off the many self-doubt-monsters and uncertainty-mongrels, that troubled me as I wrote.

To Elliot for always warming my lap, walking on my keyboard, knocking over my coffee, and making me laugh as I wrote.

To Arthur for being fat, cute, and fluffy as I wrote.

Table of Contents

A CHEAT SHEET:[1]

The following few pages will act as a condensed version of the many terms and identities found in *The ABC's of LGBT+*. I wanted the bulk of the information covered in this book to exist and be mapped out in one easy-to-access place. Each term on the cheat sheet is followed by a brief[2] definition and many of these terms can be found in the book's index. If you find a term or identity you want to learn more about, feel free to locate it in the index to find every page that term is discussed.

If you are an LGBTQIA+ terminology novice, you might consider giving these pages a once over before proceeding. Although we'll delve into more comprehensive definitions later, many of these words will be referenced right away. Having at least a basic understanding of them would be helpful. Alternatively, even if you are an LGBTQIA+ expert, you may still come across a word you are unfamiliar with before it's defined. If that's the case, come back here!

Abrosexual/romantic: Someone who experiences a fluid and/or changing orientation.

Ace: An umbrella term for any identity on the asexual spectrum. Also shorthand for "asexual."

Ace/aroflux: Someone who experiences varying degrees of attraction.

Affirm: to support, validate, and/or assert that something is true/correct.

Agender/genderless: Someone who is without gender, gender neutral, and/or rejects the concept of gender for themselves.

Ally: Someone who does not identify as LGBTQIA+, but actively supports the community.

---

1. Adorable fact: This feature of the book was inspired by my mom. She was a huge help in the editing process. However, being a straight, cisgender lady she struggled a bit with the first read through. She thought a quick "LGBTQIA+-vocab-crash-course" at the beginning might make this book more ally-friendly, and less overwhelming for newbies. Thus, this cheat sheet was born!
2. Very, very brief. Please see each term's full explanation found later in the book to get a more complete understanding of it.

Androgyne: A non-binary gender in which a person is *both* a man and woman, *neither* a man nor woman, and/or *somewhere in between* man and woman.

Androgynesexual/romantic: Someone who is attracted to androgyny.

Androgynous: Possessing qualities which are traditionally associated as *both* masculine and feminine, *neither* masculine nor feminine, and/or *in between* masculine and feminine.

Aporagender: Both a specific gender identity and an umbrella term for being a non-binary gender separate from man, woman, and anything in between while still having a very strong and specific gendered feeling.

Appropriation: Borrowing or adopting something as one's own when it did not originate from them or their culture. This type of use occurs without proper understanding, credit, and/or permission. *(Example: white people wearing feathered headdresses as costumes during Halloween.)*

Aro: An umbrella term for any identity on the aromantic spectrum. Also shorthand for "aromantic."

Aromantic: An umbrella term, or stand-alone identifier, for someone who experiences little or no romantic attraction.

Asexual: An umbrella term, or stand-alone identifier, for someone who experiences little or no sexual attraction.

Autosexual/romantic: Being able to elicit a sexual/romantic attraction from yourself by yourself and/or not desiring to partake in sexual activity with others, but still enjoying being sexually intimate with yourself.

Bicurious: Someone curious about having sexual/romantic attractions and/or experiences with more than one gender.

Bigender: Someone who has/experiences two genders.

Binary: The rigid way society divides sex and gender into only two categories: 1) male/men and 2) female/women.

Bisexual/romantic: Being attracted to two or more genders.

CAFAB/CAMAB: These are acronyms for "coercively assigned female at birth" and "coercively assigned male at birth."

Cisgender/Cis: A person whose gender identity is the same as their sex and/or gender assigned at birth.

Conflate: To confuse, blend, connect or combine two independent things/ideas.

Community: When this book uses the term "community" it refers to a collective group of LGBTQIA+ people and organizations, as well as their supporters, who are all united by common identities, cultures, and/or social goals.

Demigender: Someone who has/experiences a partial connection to one or more genders.

Demisexual/romantic: A person who only experiences attraction to people with whom they have formed a strong emotional bond.

DFAB/AFAB/FAAB: Acronyms for "designated female at birth," "assigned female at birth," and "female assigned at birth."

Diamoric: In terms of personal identity, a non-binary person may identify as diamoric to emphasize their own non-binary identity and their attraction to/relationship(s) with other non-binary people. In terms of a relationship, a diamoric relationship or attraction is one that involves at least one non-binary person.

DMAB/AMAB/MAAB: Acronyms for "designated male at birth," "assigned male at birth," and "male assigned at birth."

Enby: This is a slang term meaning "a non-binary person."

Erasure: When an identity is given insufficient representation, made invisible, or its existence is invalidated.

Female to Female/FTF: Someone whose sex and/or gender was assigned male at birth and who rejects that their gender was ever male.

Fluid: Not fixed, able to change.

-flexible: Suffix indicating someone is predominantly attracted to one gender but allows for and acknowledge exceptions. *(Example usages: heteroflexible, homoflexible, etc.)*

-flux: In regards to orientation, "flux," is a suffix that indicates that a person's attractions fluctuate in amount or intensity. *(Example usages: biflux, trifux, polyflux, etc.)*

FTM: Acronym for "female to male."

Gay: This label can refer specifically to men who are attracted to men; it can refer to people who are primary attracted to the same or similar gender as their own; or it can be an umbrella term for anyone who is not straight.

Gender: In the context of individual self, gender is the state of being a man, a woman, both, neither, somewhere in between, or something entirely different. In the context of society, gender is a system of classification rooted in social ideas about masculinity and femininity.

Gender confusion/Gender f*ck: A person who deliberately seeks to cause, or enjoys when they create, confusion in regards to their own gender.

Gender dysphoria: Distress or unhappiness experienced because one's gender does not match their sex and/or gender assigned at birth.

Gender euphoria: Extreme happiness, or comfortability, experienced because a person's gender is being affirmed.

Gender expression: The manifestation of one's gender.

Gender identity: The identifier (or lack of identifier) someone uses to communicate how they understand their personal gender, navigate within or outside our societal gender systems, and/or desire to be perceived by others.

Gender indifferent: Being gender indifferent means being apathetic about one's gender/gender expression.

Gender neutral: Having a gender that is neutral.

Gender nonconforming/Gender diverse/Gender variant/Gender-expansive: These are umbrella terms and descriptors which refer to people who identify and/or express themselves in ways that are different from society's binary norms.

Gender roles: Societal roles, positions, behaviors, and/or responsibilities allowed or expected from men and women based on societal norms.

Genderfluid: Having a gender that changes.

Genderflux: Someone whose experience with gender changes (fluctuates) in intensity.

Genderqueer: Someone whose gender exists outside of or beyond society's binary concept of gender.

Graysexual/romantic: People who experience very low amounts of attraction; people who experience attraction rarely or only under certain conditions; and/or people who are not sure whether they experience attraction.

Graygender: This identity involves having a weak sense of gender and/or being somewhat apathetic about one's gender identity/expression.

Heterosexual/romantic a.k.a. Straight: Being attracted to the other binary gender.

Homosexual/romantic: A person who is attracted to the same or similar gender(s) as their own.

IAFAB/IAMAB a.k.a. FAFAB/FAMAB: Acronyms for "intersex assigned female/male at birth" and "forcibly assigned female/male at birth."

ID: Shorthand for "identify."

Intergender: A person who identifies between or as a mix of the binary genders.

Internalization: Conscious or unconscious learning/assimilation of behaviors/attitudes.

Intersectionality: The various ways a person or group's combined social identities/roles (e.g. gender, race, socio-economic status, etc.) interact to shape their experience of the world.

Intersex: A sex category that includes people whose anatomy does not completely fit into either of society's typical definitions of male or female.

Lesbian: Women (as well as non-binary and genderqueer people who feel a connection to womanhood) who are attracted to other women.

LGBTQIA+: Stands for lesbian, gay, bisexual, transgender, queer/ questioning, intersex, asexual/aromantic, and plus for other identities that are not straight and/or not cisgender.

Male to Male/MTM: Someone whose sex and/or gender was assigned female at birth and who rejects that their gender was ever female.

Man: Someone who identifies as a man.

Masexuality/romanticism a.k.a. Androsexuality/romanticism: Attraction to men and/or masculinity.

Maverique: Someone who has an autonomous gender which exists entirely independent of the binary genders man and woman.

Maxigender: Someone who experiences many, and sometimes, all available genders to them.

Monosexuality/romanticism: Attraction to a single gender.

MTF: Acronym for "male to female."

Multigender/Polygender: Someone who has/experiences more than one gender.

Multisexuality/romanticism a.k.a. Non-monosexuality/ romanticism: Attractions to more than one gender.

Neutrois: Someone whose gender is neutral or null.

Nomasexual/romantic: Someone who is attracted to anyone who isn't a man.

Non-binary/nb: Existing or identifying outside the sex/gender binary, being neither a man nor woman, or being only partially or a combination of these things.

Normalize: to make something accepted as common or natural in society.

Norms: Behaviors society has deemed typical or standard and has come to expect.

Novosexual/romantic: A person whose attractions change based on the gender(s) they are experiencing.

Nowomasexual/romantic: Someone who is attracted to anyone who isn't a woman.

Pan/Omnigender: People who experience many, and sometimes, all genders.

Pansexual/romantic a.k.a. Omnisexual/romantic: Capable of being attracted to any or all gender(s).

Policing: The imposition of norms, or personal beliefs, by way of telling others how they should, or should not, identify, behave, or express themselves. In this book, policing is used in the context of gender and sexuality. (*Example: "You can't do ballet, you're a boy!" or "You can't call yourself a lesbian until you've dated a girl."*)

Polyamory: The practice or desire of relationships involving more than two people. Like any relationship, these require communication, honesty, and consent in order to be successful.

Polysexual/romantic: Someone who experiences attraction to multiple, but not necessarily all, genders.

Privilege: Benefits and opportunities automatically afforded to majorities or non-oppressed groups of people, that are usually unnoticed or taken for granted and occur at the expense of oppressed groups of people.

Pronouns: In this book the types of pronouns explored are words used to refer to specific people when their proper names are not being used (e.g. he, she, they, ze, e, etc.). Our society has strong associations between certain pronouns and gender.

Queer: An umbrella term or identity taken on by some LGBTQIA+ people to describe a sexual and/or gender identity that falls outside societal norms. This term has a history of being used as a slur. Although it has been reclaimed by many LGBTQIA+ people, not everyone is comfortable using it.

Questioning: Being unsure of one's sexual/romantic orientation or gender identity.

Quoisexual/romantic a.k.a. WTFromantic: A person who can't tell the difference between attractions they experience, is unsure if they experience attraction, and/or doesn't think romantic and/or sexual attractions are relevant to them.

Recipsexuality/romanticism: Experiencing attraction to someone only after knowing that they are attracted to you.

Same gender loving/SGL: This term refers to Black LGBTQIA+ people.

Self-Identification: The act of identifying a particular way, one that feels right or true for someone.

Sex: A socially constructed classification system based on a person's biology. Society typically recognizes only two sex categories, male and female, each with specific biological requirements. The reality though, is that people's biology is often more diverse than society's categories and requirements. Intersex people are an example of this.

Sex/gender assignment: Society's propensity to label an infant as male or female, man or woman, at birth, usually based on the appearance of their genitals.

Skoliosexual/romantic a.k.a. ceterosexual/romantic: People who are attracted to people of non-binary (nb) genders.

Society: The dominant community of people, laws, traditions, values, and culture in a particular area.

Spectrum: Concepts and models of identities that challenge mainstream beliefs about the rigidity of sexuality and gender. Spectrums illustrate that people can exist in the spaces between the more commonly established identities.

-spike: A suffix that indicates a person's attractions fluctuate. Spike people often feel they experience no attraction, but then suddenly and intensely experience a spike in attraction(s). (*Example usages: acespike, arospike.*)

Stigma: Negative associations and/or expectations which are tied to specific groups/labels/identities that are usually based in misconception and/or stereotypes. (*Example: Bisexuals are sometimes stigmatized as being greedy, promiscuous or confused.*)

Trans man: Someone who was assigned female at birth and is a man.

Trans woman: Someone who was assigned male at birth and is a woman.

Transfeminine: A term used to describe someone who was assigned male at birth, and who has a predominantly feminine gender and/or expresses themselves in a way they describe as feminine.

Transgender/Trans: An umbrella term for anyone whose gender identity does *not* match their sex and/or gender assigned at birth.

Transition: The process of accepting oneself and/or pursuing changes in order to affirm one's gender and/or alleviate dysphoria.

Transmasculine: A term used to describe someone who was assigned female at birth, and who has a predominantly masculine gender and/or expresses themselves in a way they describe as masculine.

Transsexual: A person whose gender is different from their sex/gender assigned at birth. Sometimes this identity is associated with having undergone and/or wanting to undergo some kind of medical transition. This is an older term that has fallen out of popular usage in favor of the word "transgender."

Trigender: Someone who has/experiences three genders.

Trisexual/romantic: Someone who experiences attractions to three genders.

Trysexual/romatic: Someone who is sexually and/or romantically open to experimenting.

Umbrella term: A word or phrase that collectively describes or refers to more than one identity/orientation/group of people. Many of the umbrella terms in this book can also double as specific, or stand-alone identities. *(Example: Genderqueer can be both a specific gender identity as well as an umbrella term which includes many gender nonconforming identities and people.)*

Validate: To acknowledge, support, and/or accept that something is real and legitimate.

Woman: Someone who identifies as a woman.

Womasexuality/romanticismm a.k.a. gynesexuality/romanticism: Attraction to women and/or femininity.

Zedsexual/romantic, a.k.a. allosexual/romantic: A person who experiences sexual/romantic attraction. (Aka someone not on the ace/aro spectrum.)

Introduction

Who is writing this book?

Hello, and welcome to *The ABC's of LGBT+*! Before we dive into the fun stuff, like what this queer-catalog-of-sorts is going to cover and why you should care, I want to take a few moments to introduce what inspired this project, and who helped make it possible.

Thirteen years ago I sat under a blanket at the foot of my bed armed with a pen and flashlight. After staring at my diary for what seemed like an eternity, I finally mustered the courage to, with tentative, shaky handwriting, come out for the very first time as "maybe, I don't know, like-liking girls sometimes."

Adorable, right? I was eleven years old, awkward, shy, and terrified of letting my secret out. As a result, I stayed closeted for seven more years and used every ounce of energy I had repressing my adolescent lady-crushes.

Hi. My name is Ashley Mardell, and some of you may know me from my YouTube channel. Online, I'm known for doing a variety of bizarre activities such as participating in drunken arts and crafts, pie'ing my fiancée in the face, and even dressing my cats up in impressive displays of drag. Among the goofy shenanigans there are a few important, underlying themes that permeate my channel. Most notably, this includes LGBTQIA+[3] visibility and education. I especially enjoy delving into the many mis- and underrepresented identities of the LGBTQIA+ world. This may be because I identify with several marginalized and misunderstood identities myself.

By the time college came around, I had finally amassed enough self-acceptance to come out beyond the pages of my diary. It took almost a year, but before we parted ways for summer break, I'd told my most important university friends (including my serious boyfriend at the time) that I was...

> ... not really into labels, but could probably fall for anyone, regardless of gender, as long as they were cool.

I was a piece of work. While a part of me desperately needed my friends to understand that I was absolutely *not* straight, another part of me would do just about anything to avoid words like "queer," "gay," or "bisexual." These terms felt contrived, confining, and frankly, scary to me. I wasn't ready to face the stereotypes and

---

3. See the cheat sheet to learn what LGBTQIA+ stands for!

stigma[4] they came with, and I wasn't sure I wanted to become a part of the community they belonged to.[5]

Then I discovered the LGBTQIA+ world on the internet, and *everything* changed. It started with only a handful of "coming out" videos on YouTube. I didn't have many LGBTQIA+ role models in my life at the time, so I let some of these online figures fill that void. It was an interesting experience. For the first time, I felt deeply connected to people because of their sexuality. I finally understood the benefits of belonging to the LGBTQIA+ community; it offered people who differed from the norm a sense of understanding and acceptance. This realization helped alleviate the nagging disconnect and subtle isolation I used to feel from the rest of world. I quickly became excited for a future of possibilities and belonging.

Aside from being refreshingly relatable, I also found these people to be impressively compassionate, caring, and supportive. They not only had a profound understanding of themselves, but also a beautiful, empathetic curiosity of others' identities. It inspired me.

I wanted to enter into this loving, open-minded network of people, and so my interest in LGBTQIA+ topics quickly escalated. Soon I found myself devouring books, blogs, documentaries, podcasts, and anything queer I could get my hands on. Never before had I known that an ocean of free LGBTQIA+ education existed, and all I had to do to access it was type a few keywords into a search bar. This abundance of new knowledge transformed me. I was no longer the hesitant, insecure, label-shy Ashley I was before. I found myself empowered, confident, and excited to take ownership of any *super gay* terminology that applied to me!

Five years, two new cats, a future wife, and a drastic short haircut later, and I'm happy to tell you this is still

---

4. See the cheat sheet for more on stigma!
5. (#InternalizedHomophobia, oops! See the cheat sheet and pages 64-66 for more on internalization!)

the case today. To be honest, I'm not sure I've ever met a person more passionate about labels and the power of language than myself. In fact, if you asked me to describe my identity in the most precise sense, I would likely say something like, "I'm Ashley, a very fluid, queer person, comfortable using the words bi, pan, and multisexual interchangeably. I'd describe my romantic orientation as demi-homoflexible and my gender as questioning, but typically existing in the spaces between woman and agender. Words I'm currently experimenting with are non-binary, gender neutral, bigender, demigirl, genderfluid, genderqueer, and genderflux. Also, I prefer to engage in monogamous relationships." Phew! Not sure what all those terms mean? Not to worry, you will soon!

In addition to my own brain and research, I am very lucky to have a team of knowledgeable experts behind me. They have fact-checked, edited, and overviewed all the information covered in this book. Some of these fabulous organizations include:

- Trans Student Educational Resources, or TSER:[6] TSER is a youth-led organization dedicated to transforming the educational environment for trans and gender nonconforming students through advocacy and empowerment. Our editor from TSER is Eli Erlick,[7] a queer trans woman, activist, and director of the organization. Her work and writing focus on trans and queer organizations, youth, education, identities, media, and pathology.

- Gender Spectrum:[8] All children and teens are affected by narrow definitions of what is permissible and appropriate for their gender. Gender Spectrum works to increase understanding of topics related to youth and gender in an effort to create more inclusive spaces for all youth. Our editor from Gender Spectrum is Executive Director, Lisa Kenney.

- *The Gender Book*:[9] This book is a fantastic gender resource which has gone on to win recognition of an IPPY award, several grants, and was selected for the 2015 Rainbow list. Our editor from *The Gender Book* is Mel Reiff. Mel is an artist and

---

6. Find more TSER here: http://www.transstudent.org
7. Find more Eli here: http://www.elierlick.com
8. Find more Gender Spectrum here: https://www.genderspectrum.org
9. Find for of the gender book here: http://www.thegenderbook.com

illustrator who created a colorful, fully-illustrated gender 101 with their friends while living in Texas.

- Everyone Is Gay:[10] Everyone Is Gay works to improve the lives of LGBTQIA+ youth using a three-pronged approach: providing honest & often humorous advice on everything from coming out to relationships to identities; talking to students across the country in an effort to create caring, compassionate school environments; and working with the families of LGBTQIA+ people to help foster an ongoing dialogue and deeper understanding. Our editor from Everyone Is Gay is the CEO and Editor in Chief of the organization, Kristin Russo.

And of course, how could anyone ever hope to make a detailed guide of LGBTQIA+ identities without a few bloggers? Personally, I view blogging spaces as unmistakable voices of the community. They have become the birthplaces of hundreds of LGBTQIA+ identities, and they are communities that constantly work on questioning, tweaking, and perfecting language to keep terms inclusive and comfortable for everyone. For these reasons, I've invited a few of my favorite LGBTQIA+ web wizards to review this book's contents. Let me introduce them:

- Vesper from QueerAsCat:[11] Vesper is a black, queer, non-binary, asexual vlogger and blogger also known as Queer As Cat on Tumblr and YouTube. Vesper strives to help raise awareness of the intersections of sexuality, gender and race and to increase visibility and representation for people like themselves who are in the crosshairs of such intersectionality.[12]

- Camille Beredjick from GayWrites:[13] Camille is a queer writer, blogger and vlogger known as GayWrites on Tumblr and YouTube. She's passionate about all aspects of the LGBTQIA+ movement and especially focuses on bisexual communities, inclusive media and journalism, and LGBTQIA+ issues in politics. She lives in New York.

- Emily Quinn from Intersexperiences:[14] Emily is an artist and animator who used to work on *Adventure Time* before she came

10. Find more Everyone Is Gay here: http://www.everyoneisgay.com
11. Find more Vesper here: http://www.queerascat.tumblr.com
12. See the cheat sheet for more on intersectionality!
13. Find more Camille here: http://gaywrites.org
14. Find more Emily here: http://emilord.com

out as intersex on MTV. Now she works full time as an activist, raising awareness for intersex issues.

- Riley J. Dennis:[15] Riley is a content creator, public speaker, writer, and activist who runs a semi-educational YouTube channel that discusses intersectional feminism, queer issues, and a host of other topics. She is a non-binary, transfeminine lesbian who is also a huge nerd. She loves Harry Potter and Pokemon.

- Pidgeon:[16] Pidgeon is a mixed Latinx, queer, genderfluid intersex person, and activist, from Chicago. They are passionate about carving out a liberation space for intersex people, especially intersex people of color. You can find them on Everyday Feminism, and on their Twitter and Facebook pages.

- Micah from Neutrois Nonsense:[17] Micah is a writer, advocate, and educator on transgender identities. Micah's site is a leading resource among the non-binary community. Micah presents humorously didactic workshops involving cookie metaphors, reluctantly talks to journalists, volunteers as a speaker at local schools, and is a closet idealist. Micah's mission is to contribute positively to everyone's experience with gender.

Hey, I'm August!

★ Trans.
★ Tall.
★ Nerdy.
★ Likes art.
★ And helping however he can.

Beyond the efforts of its reputable editors, the book also includes personal stories from approximately 40 LGBTQIA+ people who so generously donated their time and efforts to support this project. Additionally, I'd like to thank the fantastically talented, trans artist, August Osterloh for crafting the book's gorgeous illustrations.[18]

In the end, it's important that you understand that this book is truly a massive LGBTQIA+ collaborative effort.

---

15. Find more Riley here: https://www.youtube.com/c/RileyJayDennis
16. Find more Pidgeon here: http://www.pidgeonismy.name
17. Find more Micah here: http://neutrois.me
18. Find more August here: http://bit.ly/2cti1Dv

All the information has been critically reviewed by the eyes of respected organizations, online communities of everyday LGBTQIA+ people, and myself. The editors include gay, bi, ace, aro, queer, trans, intersex, and non-binary people, as well as people of color, and the personal story contributors are even more diverse! The age range of collaborators is also fairly wide, spanning from mid-teens to mid-thirties. It's my hope that the merging of these various individuals and perspectives will result in the creation of a well-rounded, ultra-detailed, LGBTQIA+ resource unlike any other out there.[19]

What is this book about?

Breaking down this book's mission is simple: It aims to be a detailed guide of many LGBTQIA+ identities and terms with an emphasis on those that are mis- and underrepresented. This book recognizes that most identities and terms have a multitude of interpretations, and it intends to cover as many as possible. Along with in-depth, written definitions, many identities and terms will also be paired with helpful infographics, links to online videos, and even anecdotes from real people[20] who claim them.

Why is this book important?

Representation of LGBTQIA+ people is grossly imbalanced. While the general public may have a basic understanding of the more common LGBTQIA+ identities like, gay and lesbian, ask a person on the street to explain something more nuanced like, maverique or genderflux[21], and you will likely be met with a blank stare.

This lack of knowledge regarding sexual and gender diversity is also largely reflected in today's media, which typically only showcases stereotyped, trite depictions of LGBTQIA+ people. Reducing us to these one-dimensional clichés is not only inaccurate, but also harmful. It perpetuates the ideas that:

---

19. However, I had the final say on which concepts made it into the book and how they were explained. Understandably, not everyone who helped edit this book agreed on every matter, so if you find yourself taking issue with anything in the text, I am who should be held accountable before the other contributors.
20. All who have nifty blogs or vlogs that you can check out if you want to learn more about them and/or their identity!
21. See pages 106 and 116 for more on maverique and genderflux!

- People are no more than their sexuality *(Example: "He's gay, that's all you need to really know.")*

- Certain behaviors and aesthetics are to be expected from individuals based on their orientation. *(Example: "Gay men are effeminate, lesbians are butch, and bi people are promiscuous. Duh.")*

- Certain behaviors and aesthetics are to be expected from individuals based on their gender identity. *(Example: "Trans women are feminine, trans men are masculine and gender neutral people are androgynous. Obviously.")*

As a result, LGBTQIA+ people who don't fit these stereotypes may not feel valid in their identities. I've heard countless stories of youth remaining closeted and confused because they didn't feel they "looked" or "sounded" enough like the "type" of person who was LGBTQIA+. They didn't believe they were "allowed" to be gay[22] and worried they'd face rejection from the LGBTQIA+ community. What's more, when all we see are stereotyped depictions, allies or people less familiar with LGBTQIA+ communities are denied interesting and nuanced looks at their fellow humans. Then, they become more likely to perpetuate the same harmful stereotypes.

From personal experience, I can tell you it's incredibly disheartening to go on a hunt for relatable, interesting LGBTQIA+ characters in TV or literature, only to find tropes such as:

- "Gay best friends" constantly preoccupied with shopping[23]

- Greasy, crude lesbians only seen in flannel[24]

- Unfaithful bisexuals convinced that their desire to experiment is a college phase

---

22. MacDoesIt made a wonderful video on this topic: http://bit.ly/2cb3FGl
23. Note: To be clear, fitting a stereotype is not inherently a bad thing. Take the person above for instance – they have a great smile and even better hair. I would be their friend in a heart beat! What becomes frustrating is when cliched depictions are the *only* portrayals of LGBTQIA+ people we see.
24. Let's be real though — flannel is amazing.

- Transgender youth isolated and rejected by their peers

- Obnoxious drag performers who only exist for comic relief

- Wounded queer heroes who bravely make it on their own after being disowned

The fact of the matter is, there are infinite ways a person can be LGBTQIA+. I eagerly await the day I'm surrounded by more realistic, complex, and empowering depictions of LGBTQIA+ people in mainstream media. Perhaps:

- A gay scientist on the asexual spectrum

- A Christian bisexual, deeply invested in his faith

- A polyamorous, trans person elected as their high school's prom king

- A non-binary bodybuilder who loves drag and takes it very seriously

- A fashion-knowledgeable lesbian helping their gender questioning friend explore gender nonconforming styles

- A popular, mixed race, intersex[25] blogger whose relationship with their father takes years of hard work and patience before any mutual love and respect is formed

Unfortunately, I fear there is a long road ahead before we see this kind of representation in mainstream media. Therefore, in an attempt to combat erasure and increase general LGBTQIA+ knowledge, this book hopes to offer visibility and a voice to identities that are usually lost and forgotten.

Who is this book for?

This book is for *anyone* interested in learning about sexual and gender diversity. That being said, as I write, I do have two target

25. See page 53 for more on what it means to be "intersex."

audiences in mind. The first is any LGBTQIA+ person who is "looking for their label." Without adequate resources or education, it's easy to be unaware of the copious identities that exist. It's also entirely possible for a person's identity to be too complex to fit any mainstream label. Not knowing how to put your identity into words can be isolating and frustrating. Used properly, language has the power to validate people's identities and grant a sense of community.[26]

On top of those searching for a label, this book is also for allies and LGBTQIA+ people looking to pack in some extra identity know-how! Knowledge is a critical part of acceptance after all. Learning about new identities broadens our understanding of humanity, heightens our empathy, and allows us to see the world from different, valuable perspectives. Additionally, these words provide greater precision when describing attractions and identities, and there is never anything wrong with having an efficient, expansive vocabulary!

How to use this book:

While this book is chock-full of labels (that hope to validate people and help them find community) it's important to note that this is meant to be a *descriptive* not *prescriptive* resource. It does not have an agenda to push labels on anyone, nor should you use it to label any individual without their consent. This book is not a weapon to police identities or place people in boxes, it's simply a catalog of

26. Vesper's story on page 108 is a great example of this!

terminology for those interested in learning about a diverse array of identities.

What's more, we should acknowledge that not everyone can agree exactly on what each identity is and how it's defined (and that's OK)! Almost every identity out there has more than one (or two, or three, or four, or twenty!) interpretations, and this book simply provides some of the most common perspectives on what each means.

Additionally, it's worth noting that public opinion of many identity labels can change over time. For example, the word "transgender" didn't come into our language until the 1960s. Before then, people often identified as "queens" or "transsexuals." Now many consider those terms offensive to describe trans people.[27] Our language and understanding of these concepts is constantly changing and that's exciting! It means people are continuing to learn and analyze!

All this being said, if you *do* happen to find a word in this book you're excited to claim, marvelous! If not, that is completely okay too. There are a variety of reasons why a person may or may not choose to label themselves. Some of these include:

- They feel too fluid to commit to one label.

- They don't think any existing label completely captures their identity.

- Their identity is still formulating and they don't want to be rushed into a qualifier.

I'm just me, and I don't really want to label myself beyond that

- They wish to avoid the stigma and/or expectations tied to certain labels.

- They don't feel they owe society an explanation as to who they are. Their identity is personal information.

27. However, some people do still identify with these terms, and if they are comfortable doing so, that's completely valid!

- They find rejecting society's propensity to classify and place everyone in boxes liberating.

- And finally, they just don't want to label themselves. It's really as simple as that. They don't want to, and they don't have to. Boom.

A person's decision to either use an identifier, or not, is completely personal, valid, and should be respected by others.

A disclaimer:

A final word of warning before we press forward: activism is tricky, and identities are complicated. It is entirely possible (and even likely) that during the course of your reading you'll find that I and/ or my team of knowledgeable collaborators have made a mistake. If this is the case, I encourage you to submit your criticism to ashleymardellbook.tumblr.com. I'll do my best to compile the critiques and comments in a nifty, online resource for those interested in learning even more. Let's embark on this journey of education together!

Part 1:

SPECTRUMS

Before we delve deeply into the details of sexual, romantic, and gender identities, let's cover my favorite topic of all, spectrums! One of the reasons I'm so fond of spectrums is because I believe, with fierce tenacity, that *nothing* in this world is black and white. Spectrums embrace gray spaces, ambiguity, and fluidity. Since these are all concepts which are integral to the human experience, I find spectrums particularly helpful in understanding and describing identity. I also chose to start the book with this section for a very particular reason; because as we learn about various identities, it's important we recognize they are not "all or nothing" concepts. Many identities can exist in various degrees and come in a range of possibilities. Remembering this is incredibly crucial as we progress.

Essentially, spectrums are tools or concepts that help us understand identities in complex ways. Often times we see them as visual aids on which we can represent and plot different identities. There are many styles, the most predominant being the linear model. This type of spectrum has two endpoints and lots of space in between. One experience frequently portrayed on a linear spectrum is *to what degree a person experiences sexual attraction.* That might look something like this:[28]

EXPERIENCE OF SEXUAL ATTRACTION

experiencing *no* sexual attraction   experiencing *lots* of sexual attraction

Decoding this visual is fairly simple. Anyone on the far left experiences no sexual attraction (**asexuality**),[29] and anyone on the far right experiences lots of sexual attraction (**zedsexuality**).[30] These plotted identities could look like the following:

---

28. There are some limitations in portraying this concept in this way. It is not perfect, and we'll learn about some other styles of spectrums later that can depict the experience of sexual attraction more accurately.

29. See page 160 for more on this

30. See page 163 for more on this

EXPERIENCE OF SEXUAL ATTRACTION

ASEXUAL
experiencing *none*

ZEDSEXUAL
experiencing *lots*

But what about people who don't feel completely asexual or zedsexual? Well, that's what all that space in the middle is for! Maybe a person feels they fall somewhere between asexual and the spectrum's mid-point. That is often referred to as **graysexuality**,[31] and one way that identity *could* look on a spectrum might be:

EXPERIENCE OF SEXUAL ATTRACTION

GRAYSEXUAL

Perhaps a person finds themselves moving all over the spectrum depending on the day and circumstance. They might identify as **aceflux**,[32] and one way that identity *could* be portrayed on a spectrum might be:

---

31. Graysexual: Someone who experiences low amounts of attractions, only experiences attraction under certain circumstances, or is unsure if they experience attraction. See page 164 for more!
32. Aceflux: Someone who experiences varying degrees of attraction. See page 169 for more!

EXPERIENCE OF SEXUAL ATTRACTION

Or maybe a person regularly experiences sexual attraction, but not a very high amount of it. That might look like this:

EXPERIENCE OF SEXUAL ATTRACTION

Interpretations of identities and the ways different people depict them, can be highly diverse. In order to represent themselves the way they feel is best, people might draw their spectrums differently. Some people might sketch brackets, plot points, doodle arrows, shade sections, and do many other things to their spectrum. In the end, there are no rules, and how a person draws their spectrum and plots themselves on it is completely up to them. Only they know how to do it best.

To give you an example, consider the following graphics. If we asked five different people who each claimed one the aforementioned identities (asexual, graysexual, aceflux, zedsexual and someone who experiences sexual attraction but not in high amounts) to each place themselves on the same spectrum, three options of how they could look, might be like the following:

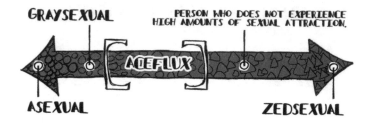

GRAYSEXUAL

PERSON WHO DOES NOT EXPERIENCE HIGH AMOUNTS OF SEXUAL ATTRACTION.

ACEFLUX

ASEXUAL

ZEDSEXUAL

Example explanations:

Asexual: "This is where I fall on the spectrum, right on the end."

Graysexual: "I used a point because my graysexuality is pretty fixed. I experience low amounts of attraction."

Aceflux: "I used a bracket to show how my aceflux identity exists between experiencing little to medium amounts of attraction."

Person who does not experience high amounts of attraction: "I simply plotted where I fall on the spectrum, just above the midpoint. I definitely experience some sexual attraction, but not a ton."

Zedsexual: "I fall on the far end of the spectrum. No part of me is asexual."

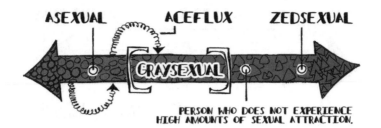

ASEXUAL   ACEFLUX   ZEDSEXUAL

GRAYSEXUAL

PERSON WHO DOES NOT EXPERIENCE
HIGH AMOUNTS OF SEXUAL ATTRACTION.

Example explanations:

Asexual: "I'm not totally at the end of spectrum. I do experience *minimal* amounts of attraction, but I still consider myself asexual."

Aceflux: "Dynamic arrows help show how intensely my attractions vary! Also, they range anywhere from zero attraction to some. I never feel more than some attraction."

Graysexual: "I can't simply plot my graysexuality with a single point. A bracket shows where my attractions exist, in a section towards the middle of the spectrum."

Person who does not experience high amounts of attraction: "I experience a bit of attraction, but sometimes I feel like it's not as much as most people. I plotted it with a point on the spectrum."

Zedsexual: "I don't think I experience attraction as much as everyone else I know, but I do experience it, and I still feel like I'm zedsexual."

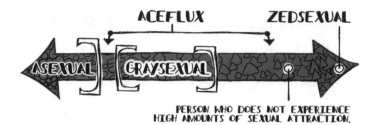

ACEFLUX · ZEDSEXUAL

ASEXUAL · GRAYSEXUAL

PERSON WHO DOES NOT EXPERIENCE HIGH AMOUNTS OF SEXUAL ATTRACTION.

Example explanations:

Asexual: "The amount of attraction I experience can vary sometimes. I never experience more than minimal amounts though, so I bracketed off the left end of the spectrum to represent my identity."

Aceflux: "I only experience two levels of attraction, and I fluctuate between them. I drew arrows pointing to those levels on the spectrum."

Graysexual: "I'm not always totally sure how much attraction I feel, but it's somewhere in the bracket I drew on the spectrum."

Person who experiences some attraction: "This dot is where I fall on the spectrum of experiencing sexual attraction."

Zedsexual: "My identity is pretty simple. I experience lots of sexual attraction so I'd plot myself on the far right."

Linear models like the ones we've been discussing so far do have some limitations however. Usually, they are too one dimensional to accurately portray all the complexities of an identity. Consider gender for instance. If you did a quick internet search of "gender identity spectrum," you would likely find hundreds of linear models with "man" and "woman" endpoints. This is because our society sees gender through a binary[33] lens and seldom recognizes identities beyond man or woman.

Society is missing out though! An abundance of genders exist that have *nothing* to do with being either a man or a woman, so it's easy to see how plotting an identity like that on a linear spectrum

33. See the cheat for more on the term "binary."

would be inaccurate. After all, placing a person between "man" and "woman" endpoints when they feel like their identity has zero relationship with either of those genders wouldn't make much sense.

An alternative to the linear spectrum model is a color wheel. Different sections of this visual represent different identities, and the merging of colors is where these identities blend. An example of just a few genders plotted on this diagram, might look like this:[34]

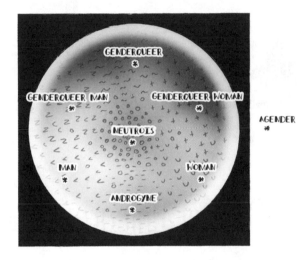

If a single point doesn't feel right, a person can instead mark multiple points, highlight whole areas, draw arrows, or do whatever they feel best represents them. For example, if someone feels they move between genders, or that they have connections to multiple genders, their color wheel might look like the following:

---

34. Don't know what these labels mean? Learn more about them in the "Gender" section, starting on page 89! Also, even after many desperate attempts, I cannot find/contact the person who originally conceptualized the gender color wheel. If you have any leads, please let me know at ashleymardellbook@gmail.com so I can give them credit.

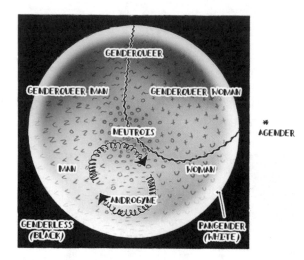

Another amazing spectrum the Trans Student Educational Resources kindly gave me permission to include in this book is the Gender Unicorn. It looks like this:

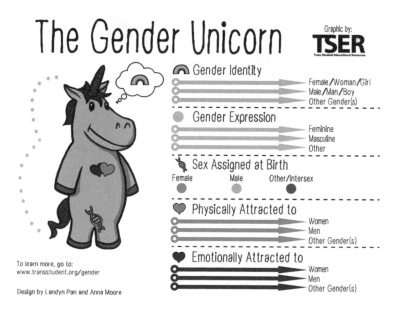

To give you an idea of how a person might utilize a spectrum like this, I've plotted my identity on the Gender Unicorn on the next page.

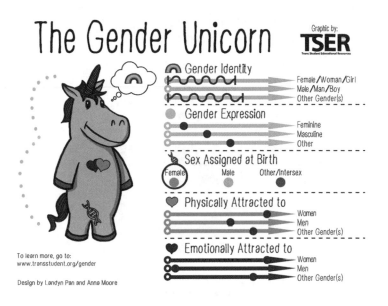

The Gender Unicorn

Graphic by: **TSER**
Trans Student Educational Resources

Gender Identity
- Female/Woman/Girl
- Male/Man/Boy
- Other Gender(s)

Gender Expression
- Feminine
- Masculine
- Other

Sex Assigned at Birth
- Female
- Male
- Other/Intersex

Physically Attracted to
- Women
- Men
- Other Gender(s)

Emotionally Attracted to
- Women
- Men
- Other Gender(s)

To learn more, go to:
www.transstudent.org/gender

Design by Landyn Pan and Anna Moore

Explanation:

My gender is fluid. Sometimes I feel partially like a woman sometimes I feel partially agender, and sometimes I feel like a simultaneous combination of both these genders.

I express femininely, masculinely, and androgynously in that order for least to greatest.

I was assigned female at birth.

I am physically attracted to many genders. However, I typically find woman attractive most often, followed by non-binary people, followed by men.

I am most often emotionally attracted to woman and non-binary people. Although it does not occur as often, I am capable of being emotionally attracted to men.

What's so cool about this spectrum is it allows you to plot *multiple* aspects of your identity on one visual. These different identity aspects include gender identity, gender expression, sex, who you're physically attracted to, and who you're emotionally attracted to. Some other concepts spectrums can model are:

- The conditions required for you to feel attraction

I'M CAPABLE OF BEING SEXUALLY ATTRACTED TO SOMEONE WHO:

Is a total stranger

I've gotten to know well and have formed a strong emotional bond

- The intensity which you experience certain identities

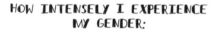

HOW INTENSELY I EXPERIENCE MY GENDER:

I feel apathetic about my gender

I experience my gender very strongly

- The intensity you experience certain attractions. These attractions might include, but are not limited to: sexual, romantic, sensual, platonic, aesthetic, and alterous attractions.[35]

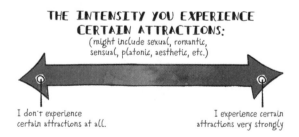

THE INTENSITY YOU EXPERIENCE CERTAIN ATTRACTIONS:
(might include sexual, romantic, sensual, platonic, aesthetic, etc.)

I don't experience certain attractions at all.

I experience certain attractions very strongly

---

35. See page 139 for more on these attractions!

- Polyamory

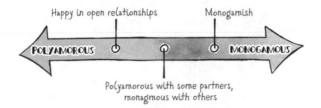

I AM:

Happy in open relationships · Monogamish

POLYAMOROUS ⟷ MONOGAMOUS

Polyamorous with some partners, monagmous with others

- And much more!

If neither a line, wheel, nor unicorn are your jam though, don't fret! You can always make your own spectral diagram that perfectly represents your sexual, romantic, gender, and any other identity in a totally custom way! Tons of people out there take this route, and some get fabulously creative. I've seen identity representations in the form of 3D spheres, planets, scatter plots, bar graphs,[36] Venn diagrams, treasure maps, and my friend, Charlie, even drew their gender as a galaxy! Check it out on the next pages.[37]

---

36. See page 117 for more on how someone might represent their identity in the form of a bar graph!
37. Find more Charlie here: http://bit.ly/2c3dVFR

Charlie's gender galaxy explanation

I never felt like my gender fit into the strict male or female binary that society had shown me growing up. After doing some research, I found that many people described gender as existing beyond the binary. They described it as a linear spectrum where you can be male, female, or anywhere in between. This felt like this was getting closer to the way I was feeling, but I still didn't feel like a mix of male and female, I felt like an entirely different gender.

Then I saw a visual representation of the gender spectrum being shown as a planet. There were uncharted lands, mountains, islands and more places than just the space between male and female. This was getting closer but still felt too finite.

To me, gender is an infinite universe. Every single person experiences gender differently. Sometimes a person has no gender, like a black hole or cluster of stars in deep space. Sometimes gender feels like a bursting colorful galaxy. Some people may stick to a strictly female planet their whole life, or jump fluidly between several. I have never been able to find a more specific label than "non-binary" that describes how I feel about my own gender, but creating the gender universe makes me feel okay about that. We all have our own unique place in the infinite gender universe.

Unless you craft your own custom diagram that is impeccably tailored to illustrate the intricacies of your identity, no spectrum model will be perfect. Many aren't able to capture the specifics, subtleties, and conditions of some identities. **Novosexuality**,[38] for example, is a sexual orientation we'll unpack more later that has several

---

38. A novosexual person is someone who's attractions change based on the gender(s) that they are experiencing. See page 158 for more on this!

contingencies and circumstances built into it. Therefore, accurately capturing it with just a few points on a spectrum is essentially impossible without some pretty lengthy footnotes.[39] It *could* look something like this:

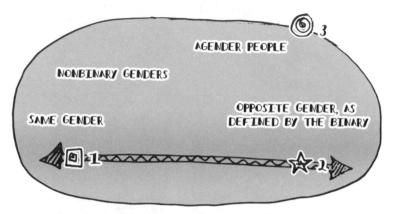

WHO I'M SEXUALLY ATTRACTED TO

 1 When I identify as a man, I am gay. I am exclusively, and very much, attracted to men.

 2 When I'm a woman I'm attracted to men. It's complicated though because I usually have to get to know a man very, very well before I feel a sexual draw to him. I'm wondering if, when I'm a woman, I'm demisexual.

 3 Sometimes I feel agender. When I identify this way gender does not play an influential role in who I am sexually attracted to. I could fall for anyone of any gender if we had a connection. This is why I have circled the entire spectrum.

As we've learned, visual spectrums find their flaws in their tendency to oversimplify identities. However, while these models are imperfect, their existence still valuably impacts the way we view identities. To show you what I mean:

---

39. I'm always a fan of a good footnote though ;)

Spectrums are dope because they:

- Challenge binaries (*Example: "Don't need gender neutral bathrooms? Everyone is either a man or woman you say? Psh, there are SO many other genders, just look at this spectrum!"*)

- Acknowledge that identities can exist in varying degrees of intensity (*I'm genderflux, and I play with colors on my spectrum to show this. On days when I feel intensely like a girl, my dot is dark purple. On days when I feel kinda like a girl, it's medium purple. On days when I feel barely like a girl, it's light purple.*)

- Allow for change and fluidity (*Example: "My identity changes so often, instead of a dot, I often draw a bracket on my spectrum!"*)

- Embrace middle spaces (*Example: "I'm Intersex. My sex is neither male nor female, but rather falls somewhere in between. I exist right around here on the spectrum."*)

- Promote inclusion within the LGBTQIA+ community (*Example: "You don't have to be gay to belong to the LGBTQIA+ community. You can also be bisexual, questioning, or many other things! There is a whole spectrum of identities that is considered LGBTQIA+!"*)

- Provide precision when describing identities, because sometimes words simply aren't enough (*Example: "Eh, I'm pretty asexual." "...What does that mean?" "Here, I'll draw where I fall on the spectrum." *quick doodle session* "OH! I see!"*)

- Remind us that the LGBTQIA+ community is more vast and diverse than we might have ever known (*Example: "Look at all these identities that fall within this gender color wheel! I haven't even heard of some! That's so cool, I want to learn more!"*)

Spectrums aren't just restricted to visual models; they can also be conceptual. Maybe something is too vast or infinite to put on a paper. Then don't! You can still *say* and *understand* that a certain identity exists on a spectrum. This simply means it can occur in varying degrees and/or come in a range of possibilities.

When it comes down to it, spectrums are simply tools and concepts available to help people describe and visualize their identities. Whether or not a person chooses to utilize spectrums is totally up to them!

PS. It is also positively okay to scribble question marks all over your spectrum – I know I did!

On the next page is a re-creation of one of my first spectrum models. (Warning: It's not perfect and perpetuates the binary. I was young, but it's cool to see how much a person can learn in just a few years!)

Ashley's 21-year-old identity spectrums:

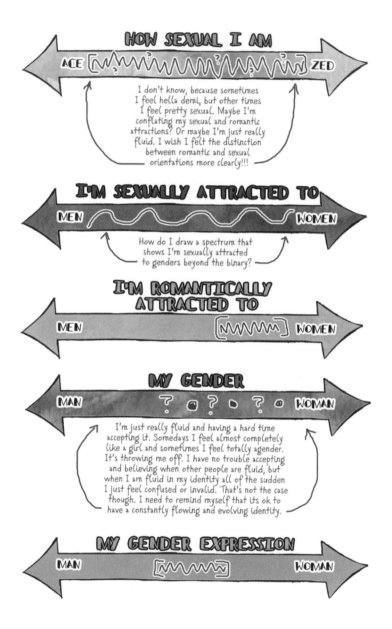

Now that we've learned so much about spectrums, you may want to take a minute to apply the information in a short exercise. In the space below consider drawing your identity spectrum as you understand it today. Remember you can make your spectrum linear, circular, spherical, or any form you like! You can also fill your spectrum with dots, shading, arrows, footnotes, question marks, doodles and more!

If you're feeling extra reflective, keep this page in mind, come back next year, and draw your spectrum in the space below again! It might be cool to see how much you and your spectrum can change over time.

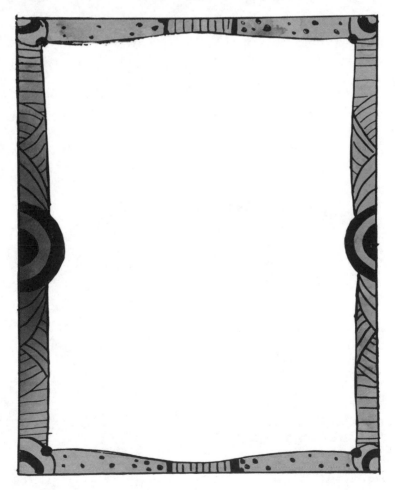

Part 2:

GENDER

CHAPTER 1:

Intro to sex and gender

Congratulations! You made it to the Gender section. Now, if you thought the cheat sheet or the spectrums section was complicated, then buckle up, because you're in for an exciting ride! Gender, in my opinion, is the most challenging concept this book will attempt to explore.

What is sex?

Because gender is so difficult to define, let's start by determining what it *isn't*: sex. So, what is sex? Let me begin by saying our culture is laden with innumerable misconceptions regarding sex. Society's definition usually goes something along the lines of,

"Either of the two main categories (male and female) into which humans and many other living things are divided on the basis of their reproductive functions." (Oxford Dictionary, 2016)

This is a common definition of sex that I'd feel safe in assuming most people are very familiar with. Something about sex I *don't* think many people are familiar with however, is that it's a social construct.[40] It's a method of classification invented by humans.

Now don't get me wrong – *our body's physicality* is not a construct. A person may, for example, have facial hair, XY chromosomes, and tons of testosterone flowing through their veins. The way our bodies *are* is simply undeniable. However, *labeling* a person like this "male", based on their physical characteristics is a human design. After all, body parts are not inherently male or female...they are just body parts.

Sex is also a system that is strongly influenced by society's binary views of gender. This is evident by the fact that society utilizes two binary sex categories that each have strong associations with the two binary genders. These two sex categories include **male** (associated with man) and **female** (associated with woman). The classification a person receives is largely based on the following:

---

40. Being a construct isn't necessarily or automatically a negative thing. There are many useful social constructs we utilize every day, like money, timekeeping, or stoplights. However, just because something is useful doesn't mean that it can't also be potentially harmful, like money for example. Some of the harmful aspects of "sex" are that it's constructed in a prescriptive, binary, and inaccurate way. That is what we will be exploring in this book.

- Chromosomes

- Hormones

- Gametes (haploid cells that fuse together during fertilization, i.e. sperm or ovum)

- Primary sex characteristics (present at birth and directly related to reproduction):

  - External sex organs (vulva, clitoral glands, penis, scrotum)

  - Internal sex organs (uterus, ovaries, epididymis, prostate gland, etc.)

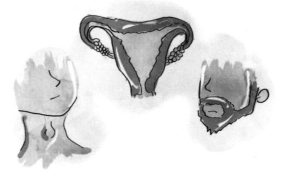

- Secondary sex characteristics (developed during puberty):

  - Body hair

  - Facial hair

  - Muscle-to-fat-ratio

  - Larynx size

  - Breasts

Society's idea of a "perfect specimen" in each of these categories might resemble the following:

"Ideal Male"	"Ideal Female"
Lots of Testosterone	Lots of Estrogen
XY chromosomes	XX chromosomes
Sperm	Ovum
Penis	Vulva
Testicles	Uterus
Facial hair growth	Little to no facial hair growth
Deeper voice	Higher voice
Broad shoulders	Broad hips
More muscular build	Breasts

But what if a person doesn't fit precisely into either side of this table? I think many of us can think of at least a few people in our lives like this. For example, do you know any men who can't grow significant facial hair? Probably. Are you friends with any women who *do* have facial hair? Perhaps.

If not, I'll introduce you to one right now: me. My face is riddled with about 10 long, dark, stray hairs. Two years ago I would have *never* admitted this. (Now I'm publishing it in a book!) I used to be very insecure of the hair on my chinny-chin-chins, but since then, I've encountered several other women who also grow facial hair. Some have random stray hairs like me, some have hairy upper lips, and some can grow beards. I see now that having some hair on your face is a natural, and not uncommon characteristic for females.

Need more examples? There are also females with broad shoulders and prominent Adam's apples, just as there are some males who grow breasts and can't produce sperm. We need to understand in many ways that while there are biological *patterns*, they are not *rules*. However, we often talk about sex (and gender) as though there are rules. Rules that if your body does not follow, deem you inferior or strange. This is something we need to start challenging and changing.

Let's take it even further, what if a person's biology looks a little more like this:

- No facial hair

- Breasts

- Genitals that resemble a vagina

- XY chromosomes

- Internal testes

- No uterus

- Little to no body hair

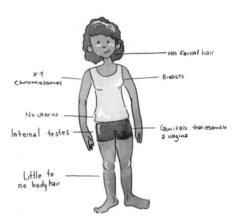

It quickly becomes more challenging to classify the aforementioned person as strictly "male" or "female". Maybe you're thinking to yourself, *"The reason we only have two sexes is because no real person actually has characteristics like the set above.[41] Or if they do, it's extremely, extremely rare. I've never met anyone like this anyway!"*

If you feel this way, you might be surprised to learn that in fact, about 1 in every 200 people is **intersex**.[42] This means they do not completely fit into either of society's ideas of what it means to be male or female. So, if your Facebook friends list is at least 200 people long you almost certainly *have* met an intersex person! To give you an even better idea of how common intersex people are, consider that 1 in every 200 is about the same as the number of natural redheads!

---

41. You may be interested to know this wasn't a hypothetical, arbitrary list of characteristics. It's actually the qualities that many intersex people with CAIS, or Complete Androgen Sensitivity Syndrome possess.
42. Statistic by the study, "Living with Intersex/DSD" by Jantine van Lisdonk https://t.co/xnY1h4lDDj

More often than not, you wouldn't know someone is intersex unless they told you. Take the aforementioned list for instance; if this individual passed you on the street, how would you know what chromosomes, hormones, or genitals they had? You wouldn't. Only their secondary sex characteristics (breasts, stature, facial structure, lack of facial hair) would be visible. And although these attributes are merely a fragment of the whole story of their sex, you'd likely flag them as a woman. Perhaps you wouldn't do this consciously. It might not be as explicit as spotting them and thinking "THEY ARE SURELY FEMALE!" But odds are, you would label them subconsciously.

This messy, haphazard sex categorization based on limited biological information occurs more than we might like to think. Millions of newborns, for instance, are hastily labeled every day. All that is required is one swift glance at their genitals, and if they most closely resemble a vulva, BOOM, the child's future as a girl has been decided with one fell swoop of the doctor's pen on a birth certificate.

Sometimes it can be hard to classify an infant's genitalia, so doctors are uncertain of which binary sex to label the child. When this happens, surgical interventions may occur. These procedures aim to physically and hormonally alter people's bodies in order to provide them with "more socially acceptable sex characteristics."[43] As we learn more about sex and gender however, people are speaking out against these surgeries with the hope that medical providers and guardians give their children the autonomy to choose what happens with their anatomy. Here is Claudia to share some of her feelings on these surgeries.[44]

I'm Claudia, and I'm an intersex person! Intersex people are those with a combination of traits that are traditionally considered "male" or "female" – and sometimes traits atypical for either – in the same body. Because our bodies aren't easily categorized as male or female, being intersex is often characterized as a medical condition that needs to be "fixed." As a result, parents and clinicians regularly opt to perform surgeries and other procedures to cosmetically alter our bodies to look like "normal" boy or girl bodies.

These procedures don't benefit our health, are performed without our consent, and may result in lasting physical, psychological, and/or emotional harm. It's strange for me to think about parents and doctors choosing to arbitrarily remove other body parts that are healthy and working perfectly fine – say, the pinky finger on the left hand. If people found out about a society that routinely removed baby's left pinky fingers shortly after birth, we would likely be horrified. It would make big headlines, get grabbed by the news cycle – most people would probably

43. Like characteristics from the "Ideal male/Ideal female" chart on page 52
44. Find more Claudia here: http://bit.ly/2cxBJwT

think this was completely bonkers and not okay, right? But when parents and doctors choose to remove body parts from intersex babies and children, many societies think it's for our own good, that they're helping us. They're not.

Everyone should have the right to bodily autonomy – to literally be able to choose what body parts we have and choose to keep or modify. Taking that right away from intersex kids isn't okay, and intersex activists are working to end these practices.

Not every intersex person undergoes surgery, and many have external sex organs that resemble "typical male" or "typical female" genitalia. As a result, these people might not learn until puberty, or even later in life, that they are intersex. Some never learn at all. Sometimes, even those who do undergo nonconsensual surgery are kept in the dark!

Learning that one's biology is different than they expected can be a surreal, confusing experience. Due to our culture's intense focus on a strict gender binary, sometimes intersex people can feel incomplete, shameful or alone. This is why I would argue that viewing sex in a non-binary way is, more factually accurate and healthier.

One way that some people conceptualize sex in a non-binary way, is by viewing it on a spectrum. These spectrums might look something like the following:

This is a spectrum where intersex falls between male and female. A person can fall anywhere on this spectrum. For instance, they could be male, somewhat male, intersex, somewhat female, or female.

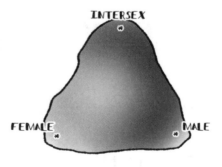

This spectrum is in a triangular shape because some people feel that being intersex is not "in between" male and female, but rather a sex that is entirely different. Also, some feel placing intersex between male and female implies that intersex is an incomplete sex.

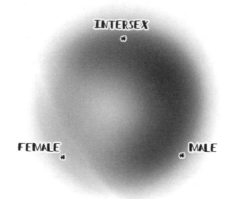

In this spectrum there are no endpoints. It communicates that sex is infinite. The kinds and combinations of characteristics our bodies can have is too vast and diverse to put boundaries on.

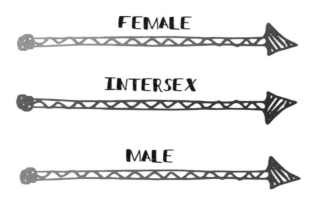

This spectrum communicates that it's possible to have a combination of characteristics that make our sex simultaneously male, female, and/ or intersex.

Or perhaps sex exists purely as a conceptual spectrum without visual illustrations. The number of biological combinations that can occur in different people's bodies is vast and full of possibility. Maybe simply recognizing that, rather than finding a visual way to model it, is enough.

Others feel that viewing sex on any spectrum genders body parts and characteristics that aren't inherently gendered and conglomerates a specific set (usually the "male" and "female" sections of the spectrums) as "natural" or "normal." Everything in the middle on the other hand, feels implied to be incomplete or imperfect. People who feel this way often feel that sex should not be assigned at birth to begin with.

No matter what you think the correct way to view sex is, it's undeniable that there is more than just male and female. When it comes to sex, our bodies are complex and beautifully diverse. This is why sex is most definitely not a binary thing; it is more than:

In our culture however, people are *constantly* forced to box themselves into one of the only two mainstream options offered. A person's sex is referenced on government forms, identification documents, medical papers, voting ballots, test questionnaires, dating sites, applications, and in some places even bathrooms are divided by a person's "sex at birth." It is impossible to escape society's binary view of sex. We are all forced to face it whether or not we subscribe to or fit into it.

This is a problem because as we've established, not everyone meets society's requirements for being "male" or "female." Being repeatedly forced to misidentify their sex and/or rarely being acknowledged, can cause intersex people to feel isolated, invalid, and erased. This is why we need to reevaluate the way we view sex and start making space for people who do not totally fit into the typical "male" or "female" boxes. These people do exist and their sex is not inferior to anybody else's.

What is gender?

I have rewritten this subsection 114 gazillion times (approximation). I'll be frank; gender is complicated, and honestly I'm still working on my understanding of it. I believe very few people out there have *total* comprehension of the concept, and I don't think anyone is *the authority* on gender. I know I'm certainly not, so it's important to me that I preface this chapter by saying that our knowledge of gender is expanding every day, and every individual creates their own understanding of what gender is. Yours may be different from mine.

There is no universal agreement on the definitions of many of these terms, and I am only one voice, so please don't take my word as "gender law." I encourage you to think critically and for yourself. That being said, I've done my best to develop and gather my thoughts into what you'll hopefully find is a helpful guide to gender. Let's get into it!

One of the reasons gender is so hard to perfectly and completely define, is because the word has a few meanings, based on the context it's being used within:

In the context of *individual self*, "gender" can be defined as:
The state of being a man, a woman, both, neither, somewhere in between, or something entirely different.

Example: *"My gender is neutrois."*

In the context of *society*, "gender" can be defined as:
A socially constructed system of classification which typically perceives people as one of two binary genders -- man or woman -- and assigns a set of cultural expectations of roles, behaviors, expressions and characteristics to each person based on that classification.

Example: *"Welcome to 'Generic Clothing Store.' Our clothing is divided by gender. The 'girls section' is over there, the 'boys section' is over there."*

Let's first break down the definition of gender in the context of individual self: *"The state of being a man, a woman, both, neither, somewhere in between, or something entirely different."*

We can start better understanding what this means by noting that gender, in comparison to sex, is significantly less tangible. Nothing physical about a person (chromosomes, hormones, genitals, the clothes they wear, etc.) dictates their gender. Instead, gender is composed of self-understanding and self-perception. In the simplest terms: assigned sex is rooted in our biology, while gender is rooted in who we know ourselves to be beyond our biology.

In this line of thinking, no gender is invalid.[45] Someone might be a binary gender (i.e. man or woman), they could be non-binary[46] (i.e. neither man nor woman, multiple genders simultaneously, flowing between genders, etc.), or they could be without gender. We'll dive into the specifics of these different terms soon, so don't panic if you don't know what they mean yet! What's important to understand is that there are no rules as to which gender is right or wrong. Also, no gender is inherently more natural or legitimate than any other. This is because a person's gender is their truth.

Now, let's backtrack a bit and address the definition of "gender" in its societal context:

"A socially constructed system of classification which typically perceives people as one of two binary genders -- man or woman -- and assigns a set of cultural expectations of roles, behaviors, expressions and characteristics to each person based on that classification."

While earlier I said gender has no rules, in the same breath, I acknowledge that, as far as society is concerned, gender is riddled with rules and pressures. Our culture is constantly thrusting gender expectations on all of us. This becomes a problem when it limits people's expressions and identities and perpetuates intolerance of anything that's not the norm.

So the question then is; how *does* society view gender? I'm sure it's no surprise that the answer is; usually in a very binary way, as either man or woman. A "man" is associated with our culture's idea of what "male biology" is (a penis, XY chromosomes, etc.) and a "woman" is associated with our culture's idea of what "female biology" is (a vagina, XX chromosomes, etc.). This is the first gender norm society thrusts upon us; that to identify as a particular gender, we must have a particular anatomy.[47]

Gender norms are not just about our bodies though; they are all the standards deemed appropriate by society, for men and women. These can include:

· How intelligent men and women can be

---

45. However certain gender labels can be appropriative, harmful, and/or problematic.
46. See page 109 for more on non-binary genders!
47. Often society will even go beyond mere associations between gender and biology. Sometimes they will confuse them entirely or incorrectly use "sex" and "gender" synonymously.

- How much money men and women should make

- The clothes men and women should wear

- How men and women's bodies/hair should look

- What men and women should be interested in

On top of gender norms, our society also has many gender roles. **Gender roles** are societal roles, positions, behaviors, and/or responsibilities allowed or expected from men and women based on societal norms. Societal gender roles for men and women can include, who is the:

Breadwinner	Fashionista
Nurturer	Initiator
Bookkeeper	Housekeeper
Negotiator	Planner
Cook	Protector
Athlete	One-who-unclogs-the-toilet

To give you an idea of how gender is viewed in our culture today, here's a depiction of society's ideal man and woman, who subscribe to many of correct gender roles and norms:

It's likely many of us do not *totally* identify with either figure, nor do we believe a person must possess each and every one of those qualities in order to correctly portray a man or woman. We might even deny the binary entirely and acknowledge the infinite number of genders that truly do exist.

However, even if we are able to do this, we are still going to be influenced by society's binary and traditional views. This is understandable. These ideas have become ingrained and internalized within us from an early age. From separate bathrooms, to gendered clothing, to almost exclusively cis[48] representation in media, these are the realities we face every day. We have been conditioned to accept society's binary, traditional views. Unless we are incredibly self-aware and practiced in the art of unlearning, chances are we are influenced by our culture's views of gender on, at least some level. This can impact the way we see others' genders, as well as our own.

My friend Kai is an excellent example of this. Being a trans man,[49] he's had extensive practice challenging the binary and defying gender roles. He came out almost two years ago, and has since learned to love himself and cultivate a strong sense of trans pride. All this being said, even Kai struggles with internalized transphobia[50] from time to time.[51]

48. See page 90 for more on the term "cis/cisgender."
49. See page 98 for more on trans men.
50. Transphobia: beliefs and misinformation about transpeople that can result in bias, mistreatment, neglect, invalidation, systemic discrimination and violence against them.
51. Find more Kai here: http://bit.ly/2c9D1i0

In regards to internalized transphobia, I do believe that this is an issue I've dealt with, specifically when it comes to the perception of my own body. The odd thing is; despite my opinion that body parts do not coordinate with gender, I still struggle viewing trans people as "normal" sometimes. I believe this comes from the way I was conditioned to view bodies and normality.

I think that everyone, regardless of identity, struggles with having their opinions influenced by media and society. Personally, I sometimes have ideas or opinions in my head that do not match how I feel in my heart. For example, due to my upbringing, I sometimes fail to see trans people as their valid gender. Although this is not how I feel in my heart, and it's not anything I would express out loud, this idea is still stuck in my head. One of my favorite quotes regarding this matter is, "We have two ideas that pop into our heads when forming an opinion, the first idea is what we are conditioned to think, the second idea is what determines who we are as people."

Overall, I still feel odd about myself and about my trans identity. I am still un-stitching the rules I was taught about gender. I think this is an issue that lots of trans people face; our community, like many others, has to work very hard to find self-acceptance, especially after years of cis-normative conditioning.

I appreciate Kai's willingness to be vulnerable and share his struggles. Don't worry if you've ever felt like this, you're not alone. Many people battle with shaking the ideas society has taught them about gender. It's a hard mission to complete.

The good news though, is that even though these ingrained, traditional ideas of gender are hard to totally rid ourselves of, it's something we can work on! Some good practices for deconstructing and reconstructing our ideas of gender include:

- Try to not assume a person's gender or pronouns when first meeting them. Instead consider asking them what pronouns they use, or use gender neutral pronouns until told otherwise.

- Realize that objects (clothes, deodorants, haircuts) don't have genders, and gendering these items can perpetuate traditional and binary gender roles/ideas.

- Dialogue, dialogue, dialogue! The more we (respectfully) converse and ask questions about gender, the more we (and the people we're chatting with) will learn! Having these conversations also helps normalize[52] these topics and works to remove the stigma around them.

- Be brave and speak up, even if it's uncomfortable.[53] It can be scary, but if you or a friend are faced with cissexism[54] or cisnormativity,[55] consider saying something. Standing up and advocating can be a very empowering experience, and it also help inform those who still have some learning to do.

- On the flip side, realize that *you* almost certainly still have a lot to learn about gender. You become markedly less able and prone to absorb knowledge if you already think you're an expert. One way you can do this is by making space for non-cis people to speak about their experiences.

- Accept that becoming vastly knowledgeable and informed about gender is not going to happen overnight. The process is an ongoing one that takes constant, *active* effort.

52. See cheat sheet for more on what it means to "normalize" something.
53. Be sure to only do this if it's safe!
54. Cissexism: A form of sexism in which cisgender people are viewed as normal, right, and best.
55. Cisnormativity: The assumption that all, or nearly all, people are cisgender.

- Fight for representation in media. This could mean something simple like, talking about "how cool it would be to have a bigender character" on the forums of your favorite show's website, or something more involved like, starting your own webcomic with a non-binary protagonist!

- Seek out and listen to people whose experiences are different from your own. Hearing diverse gender perspectives will broaden your knowledge of existing experiences and increase your empathy.

- Actively question what we are doing and why. Rather than passively consuming our culture's ideas and representation of gender, break them down. Reflect on why they are the way they are. Greater understanding comes through analysis.[56]

- Encourage freedom of gender expression.[57] This could mean playing or experimenting with your own gender expression, or noticing a friend who is expressing in a gender nonconforming way, and saying, "HEY PAL! You look flippin' lovely!"

By this point we have learned a *lot* about the word "gender." We've learned about what it means in the context of *individual self* and in the context of *society*. We've learned that gender can be complex, multi-faceted, and a different experience for everyone. Basically we've learned that gender is a collage of many things. In every sense and context of the word gender is:

56. This video by the lovely Alex Bertie is a great example of this: http://bit.ly/2chA4hf
57. See page 73 for more on gender expression!

GENDER IS:

That folks, is gender in all it's amazing complex, beautiful glory. Next let's learn a little about "**gender identity**." Often, "gender identity" is the coming together of many, or all, of the above elements into an identifier that communicates how someone:

· Understands their personal gender

- Navigates within or outside our societal gender systems

- Desires to be perceived by others

Once we understand how these different elements come together, we form a concept of self and we often try to find the language and/or label that best conveys that concept. That's gender identity. **It's how an individual perceives their gender(s) and the word(s) they use to communicate that to others.**

Great, you now have an understanding of both the terms "gender" and "gender identity." Next, let's talk about how to use them. This is important because there is a disparity in our culture's language that can make non-cis people feel like their genders aren't taken seriously.

Consider how we *rarely* hear the term "gender identity" used when referring to cis people. On the flip side, consider how *frequently* we hear "gender identity" in reference to trans and non-binary (nb) people. Probably, much more than we ever hear the simple word "gender." "Gender identity" is used *so often* in reference to trans/nb people in fact, that sometimes it seems to be the *only* phrase our society uses when talking about trans/nb people's genders.

Situations like this are understandable since the terms "gender" and "gender identity" do certainly have some overlap. For many people their gender and gender identity are one in the same.[58] It's important to understand though, that consistently tacking on the word "identity" for trans/nb people (when society doesn't do this for cis people) can make us feel like our genders are somehow fabricated or debatable options. It can be very discouraging and invalidating.

58. An example of someone who's gender and gender identity haven't always aligned could be my friend Jake. Jake came out as a trans man just recently. Although he is a man, and has always been a man, if you would have asked him what his gender identity was a few years ago he would have said "woman." At that time, his gender identity did not reflect his true gender.
One of this book's editors, Mel, shared another a story with me that also reflects non-aligning gender and gender identities. They said, "When I was six, if you'd asked me what my gender was, I'd say I was a girl. That was my gender identity (the label I best knew to describe myself). Later, I learned an identity word that fit better (tomboy) and realized retrospectively that my gender had in fact been tomboy all along."

We see this even more often in verb form. The word "identify" is frequently thrown around in ways that diminish the validity of trans/nb people's genders:

It's almost as if trans/nb people don't have genders in the exact same way cis people do. They just have their assigned sex and then their "gender identity." Cis people, however are consistently referred to as having "genders." This can be frustrating because it insinuates that non-cis people's genders are less legitimate or inherent than cis people's.

So what do we do? When used properly, both "gender" and "gender identity" are powerful terms. We all need to start paying attention to *when* and *how* we use these terms. We can do this by asking ourselves a few questions: Are "gender identity" and/or "identify" words that I only/consistently use when talking about trans/nb people? Do I ever using the phrase "gender identity" to replace the word "gender" when talking about trans/nb people? On the flip side am I always describing cis people as having "genders" rather than "gender identities?"

If your answers to any of the above questions are yes, you may want to re-evaluate your usages. Using *both* terms (as opposed to just "gender identity") to refer to trans/nb people can help trans/nb people feel their identities are being taken as seriously as cis people's. Additionally, using *both* terms (as opposed to just "gender") when referring to cis people can help remind cis people of the fact that their genders are identities as well. They are not more natural or inherent than trans/nb people's.

Gender expression:

Next let's explore gender expression. **Gender expression** is the manifestation of one's gender. It's a person having a sense of their gender and expressing it. This can include, but is not limited to, elements like clothing, language, body language, voice, name, smell, pronouns,[59] cosmetics, art, decor, and hairstyle. Gender expression can be private:

· Thinking to yourself in a certain voice.

· Painting your toenails even though you plan to cover them with shoes.

· Wearing certain undies no one sees but you.

· Playing a video game by yourself and picking an avatar that matches your gender/uses your desired pronouns.

Or public:

· Choosing a masculine name you share with people.

---

59. See page 81 for more on this!

- Styling and/or growing out your hair a feminine way.

- Wearing certain colognes/perfumes you feel match your gender.

- Putting on a combination of clothes that are both feminine and masculine in hopes people read you as androgynous.[60]

Often people use their gender expression to communicate their gender to others. It cues people in to how we'd like to be perceived and the language people should use when referring to us. For some individuals, gender expression is very important. Expressing their gender in the right way can help them:

- Feel connected to and affirmed[61] in their gender *(Example: "Wearing lipstick helps me feel like a woman. It's glossy, bright, feminine, and I mean, if I wasn't meant to wear it, then why do I look so damn good?!")*

60. See page 118 for more on the term "androgynous."
61. See cheat sheet on to learn more about the term "affirm."

- Feel natural *(Example: "All my life people expected and pressured me to dress 'like a boy.' Now that I've accepted myself, I wear whatever I want. No more 'boy clothes' that feel like costumes. I'm neutrois, and I organically gravitate towards androgynous clothes, so that's what I wear!")*

- Alleviate dysphoria[62] *(Example: "I'm unhappy with my body, but sometimes I sit down and draw what I think the real me looks like, and it makes me smile.")*

- Be perceived by others as the correct gender *(Example: "When I dress like a boy people usually use 'he/him' pronouns and it's the best feeling ever!")*

- Feel liberated from social pressures and expectations. *(Example: "I'm genderfluid.[63] Understanding my gender can feel like a roller coaster and still trying to adhere to society's expectations can be exhausting. One day I decided to throw those pressures out the window and wear whatever the heck I found CUTE. I can't tell you how empowered and free I've felt since! Only I control how I look, no one else gets a say.")*

As mentioned earlier, society has countless ideas about how different genders "should" express and present. This is why so many products out there are "gendered." I've seen everything from clothing, cosmetics, razors, earbuds, sunscreen, pens, bookmarks, candles, beer, to even *sandwiches*, all gendered in stores! When stores divide products into binary gendered sections, they place a great amount of implicit pressure on how particular genders should shop and express themselves.

---

62. See page 92 for more on "dysphoria."
63. See page 114 for more on the term "genderfluid."

...really? For men? It's a BURGER. How can food be gendered? WE ALL EAT? Asdfghjklsdfg...

This is where I can't help but get on my soapbox. Personally, it feels ridiculous to me that a company or brand can decide, for all of us, that an inanimate object has a gender. I tried to gather my thoughts into a somewhat clear and concise rant, but I became too heated and ended up with tangential, infuriated ramblings. Thus, I give you Rowan. Rowan is a fellow online content creator who has a particular knack for intelligently and articulately critiquing things through queer feminist lenses.[64]

Give people a baby-gender-reveal and suddenly they become fortune tellers.

"It's a boy?! He'll be kicking a ball around in no time! He'll be a little Casanova like his daddy!"

"It's a girl?! I bet mum's pleased, she'll be so cute! Dad won't need to worry until she brings home a boyfriend!"

The growing tradition of elaborate and public gender reveals might seem like a simple, cute way to celebrate a pregnancy milestone, but historians

---

64. Find more Rowan here: http://bit.ly/1TSQ7oB

like Jo B. Paoletti think there's more to it than that. Knowing the gender of your child before they pop out allows you to start buying gendered products earlier than ever.

Before your bundle of joy makes its way into a delivery room, your baby more than likely already has clothes, toys, mobiles, and nursery decorations bought for them by you, your friends, and family. According to Paoletti, this technological advancement of being able to predict a child's gender, that came about in the 1980s, fed through to marketers and manufacturers, who lapped up the chance to sell gender divided products to proud parents-to-be.

This cornucopia of pink or blue, dolls or trucks, nurses or doctors, princesses or monsters, that greets a child from their first moments, creates a binary framework that continues through their lives.

Perhaps it seems natural or harmless on the surface, but in news that might shock some people, pink is not inherently a feminine color. In fact, less than 100 years ago it was seen as the height of masculinity. All that gendered products do– from science kits for boys, to makeup kits for girls, to Bic's lady pens, to the pink tax that makes women's products more expensive than men's – is limit people's experiences and their understanding of gender.

When gender neutral parenting, or discussing the arbitrary nature of the gender binary is brought up, people are often accused of "shoving an agenda down kids' throats." But what people fail to see is that the "norm" itself is an agenda, and at least deconstructing the binary is one with the freedom to choose beyond imposed and meaningless limitations.

In the end, we shouldn't let society pressure us to express in any certain way. We can dress, sound, smell however we like.

For some, looking like a girl might mean this:

For others, it might mean this:

There may also be complex and varied reasons people decide to express in certain ways. Safety, dress codes, parental pressure, wanting to be taken seriously, money, access, culture, religion, and numerous other factors, can also play into a person's expression. Riley talks about some of the factors that influence her gender expression on the following page.[65]

_____

65. Find more Riley here: http://bit.ly/2ctjXfs

My gender expression honestly changes a lot depending on who I'm around. As someone who was assigned male at birth, I have more masculine features, so presenting in a feminine way can be dangerous for me. It's one thing to receive dirty looks or have things whispered about you as you walk by, but trans women, especially those who are outwardly visible as trans, are more likely than other people to physically beaten or killed. Knowing this, my gender expression tends to be more masculine and normative than I would always like it to be, mostly as a defense mechanism.

However, when I do have the opportunity to present as I want, I tend to prefer things that are typically associated with being feminine: eyeliner, racerback tank tops, sweatshirts that hang off one shoulder, yoga pants, short shorts, boots, etc. Wearing those things makes me feel comfortable because then I feel like people are perceiving me more like the way I perceive myself. However, I don't think they're necessary to my identity — I'm the same regardless of what's on my body.

The main way I've generally felt a bit different in this sense from other trans women (and maybe part of the reason I like the label "non-binary") is that I never felt an intense urge to change my name, take hormones or get surgery. Obviously, there's nothing wrong with trans people who do feel that way — it just wasn't my experience, and for a while, I didn't think I would ever do any of that. At this point, I've decided to medically transition in the near future, but for me, that's mostly so other people can see me the way I really am. So I can be safe and present myself how I want.

Riley also brings up another interesting aspect of gender expression and presentation: how others perceive us is not always in our control. We often talk about expression as being the public part of our gender, how we communicate our gender in the world we live in. This includes both what we are trying to communicate, as well as things we may not be intentionally communicating but that are read by others anyway. For instance, even when Riley presents in a feminine way, she acknowledges that some people may still perceive her as a man. This just goes to show that appearance and gender, are not one in the same.

Based on her story we can tell that gender expression is clearly something Riley has thought about a lot. This isn't the case for everyone though. Some people choose to wear certain clothes, makeup, or perfume for reasons that have nothing to do with gender. They may not feel a connection between their presentation and their gender. They also may be indifferent about which gender others perceive them as. This is completely valid as well. AJ is someone who is somewhat indifferent about their gender expression.[66]

Growing up, I never really identified with any certain type of "style". When I was 14, my friend introduced me to the world of skirts. I was so into it. I never saw it as me bringing out my femininity though; I just saw it as "Hey. I look pretty cute in this!" That was my skirt phase.

Two years later, I found myself more and more interested in button ups and androgynous clothing. At this point in time, I was also educating myself more about gender. It was a new concept to me. I thought heavily about my gender whenever I put clothes on, because subconsciously I was giving into gender roles, labeling my androgynous clothing as "boy clothes" and my skirts as "girl clothes".

It was a confusing time. I'd wear androgynous clothes, and still feel just as "girly" as before. I'd wear "feminine" clothes, and still feel just as "manly" as before. The more I thought about gender, the more I put my clothes into binaries. I assumed that the gender I presented through my clothes had to correlate with the gender I identified as, and that would be my "gender expression."

Soon, I realized that I was putting an unnecessary stress on clothes and I said "Screw it. Let me wear what I want!" Recently, I cut my hair short

---

66. Find more AJ here: http://bit.ly/2cxCaXO

just because. I'd never had it short and wanted to try something new!
Nowadays, I just refer to it as "expression," and not "gender expression"
because I don't necessarily think clothes or hair have anything to do with
my gender.

To conclude, gender expression is a complex matter. Sometimes it's indicative of a person's gender, sometimes it's not. Every individual gets to decide for themselves how they want to express and what the relationship is between their expression and their gender.

Pronouns:

Many languages have "grammatical gender." "Grammatical gender" is simply a noun class system. It divides nouns into different groups and provides a system of agreement between them and other kinds of words (e.g. adjectives, articles, pronouns, verbs, etc.) Some languages gender everything, even words for objects that don't have strong cultural associations with masculinity or femininity. In French for example, chairs are feminine and airplanes are masculine. This is a great illustration of how a word's grammatical gender has less to do with actual *gender,* and more to do with having a set of rules for categorizing and forming agreements between words.

Unlike many other languages around the world, modern English actually has no grammatical gender. This may surprise people seeing as many pronouns have strong gender associations. These associations however, are purely a social, not grammatical one.

Speaking of pronouns, let's define what they are. **Pronouns** are words used to refer to nouns when not specifically using the noun's proper name. Two of the most common pronouns utilized to refer to people include:

Pronoun Family	Subject Pronoun	Object Pronoun	Possessive Determiner	Possessive Pronoun	Reflexive Pronoun
He	He	Him	His	His	Himself
She	She	Her	Her	Hers	Herself

In English society typically associates "he" with men, and "she" with women. Because of this, pronouns are often used as a form of gender expression for some people. Using the correct pronouns can help some people feel affirmed in their gender because they are being perceived and referred to in a way they feel represents them. This is why pronouns can be so important for some people. However, a person's pronouns can also have nothing to do with their gender. (Not sure why a person might choose to use pronouns unrelated to their gender? Hang tight! We'll dig into that soon!)

Now let's look at one of the most common "gender neutral" pronouns:

Pronoun Family	Subject Pronoun	Object Pronoun	Possessive Determiner	Possessive Pronoun	Reflexive Pronoun
They	They	Them	Their	Theirs	Themselves

There are many reasons someone might use "they" pronouns. One possibility being that "they" does not imply any information about a person's gender. Therefore, if someone identifies as "gender neutral" or wishes to keep their gender ambiguous, "they" could be a good pronoun option for them.

There is a common misconception that "they" is used exclusively to refer to plural nouns, and cannot be used in a grammatically correct singular sense. This is untrue. So untrue, in fact, that the American Dialect Society, a 127-year-old, well established organization, named "they" its 2015 Word of the Year. It wasn't any old usage of "they" that was being honored though; it was specifically the singular, gender neutral version of the word. As in, "I have a stellar friend named Caden. They are very cool and currently questioning their gender. They rock!" The tribute to this pronoun was truly a momentous occasion! Because, hey – if over 300 grammarians and linguists testify that "they" is a valid gender neutral, singular pronoun option, who can really argue?

For people who don't want to use "they" but are still looking for a gender neutral pronoun, there are several other awesome pronoun options. These include:[67]

e/em/eir/eirs/emself

ey/em/eir/eirs/eirself

ey/em/eir/eirs/emself

hir/hir/hir/hirs/hirself

xe/hir/hir/hirs/hirself

xe/xem/xyr/xyrs/xemself

xe/xim/xis/xis/xirmself

xe/xir/xir/xirs/xirself

xie/xem/xyr/xyrs/xemself

zay/zir/zirs/zirself

ze/hir/hir/hirs/hirself

ze/zir/zir/zirs/zirself

ze/zan/zan/zans/zanself

zed/zed/zed/zeds/zedself

zed/zed/zeir/zeirs/zeirself

zhe/zhim/zhir/zhirs/zhirself

zhe/zhir/zhir/zhirs/zhirself

zie/zir/zir/zirs/zirself

So far we've explored a multitude of pronoun options, and we've acknowledged society's associations between these pronouns and masculinity/femininity.

All this being said, it's important to note that people can use whichever pronoun they wish to honor themselves. After all, pronouns are simply communication tools which are meant to best represent the person they are referring to. Thus if someone feels a certain pronoun is the best fit for them, they should use it, even if it opposes social norms. This means trans men can use "ze" pronouns, genderfluid[68] people can use "she" pronouns, and demigirls[69] can use "he" pronouns, and so on.

At first I had a hard time comprehending why a person might choose to use pronouns that defy social norms. Then a friend shared an analogy with me that made a lot of sense.

---

67. A very cool site called the "Pronoun Dressing Room" allows you to try on and experiment with several different pronouns: http://bit.ly/2cGrB59
68. See page 114 for more on what it means to be genderfluid.
69. See page 104 for more on what it means to be a demigirl.

Pronouns are like any form of gender expression. Take clothes for instance; although society has an endless number of rules and expectations regarding what people of certain genders should and shouldn't wear, you can still try on anything you like. You might find certain clothing is a good fit and "feels right" on you even if it was "meant for another gender." This shouldn't stop you from wearing it though.

The reason some individuals wear "differently gendered" clothing isn't always because it "feels right." Some people do it because gender-bending is fun, and to them the division of expression into two rigid categories seems arbitrary and confining. A trans man for example might wear clothing from the "women's section" because, "Why the flip not? All these expectations regarding what guys are supposed to wear are silly. I'm going to actively dissociate from them in my presentation!"

This entire clothing analogy can be applied to pronouns. After all, for many of us pronouns are a form of gender expression and there is no "correct way" for one to express their gender. Tori is a fantastic example of someone who doesn't conform to pronoun norms. Her gender is non-binary, she uses she/her pronouns, and here she is to explain why.[70]

70. Find more Tori here: http://bit.ly/2cb5bIp

When I think about my own gender, consistency is null. On some days, I wear dresses and wonder if I'll ever surgically remove my breasts; on others, I wear bowties and wonder why, if womanhood feels so hellish, manhood doesn't feel like the heaven I once thought it would be. What remains the same in my conception of my gender is a sense of queerness — that is, strangeness, peculiarity, deviation from the norm.

This is not to say that I believe genderqueerness to be abnormal. In fact, I would argue that it is a very common experience. Genderqueerness, as I define it personally, simply means an experience with gender that is queer, that creates a cognitive dissonance between one's intrinsic identity and the values and expectations of their society.

For me, pronouns play no role in this self-conception. In fact, I find myself quite nonchalant about them precisely because they are indicators of a highly gendered society in which I feel I have no place. Thus, I find myself using she/her/hers pronouns not because "it feels right," as is the case in many people's experiences, but simply because it is convenient. When most people see me, they will not ask about pronouns; they will call me a girl and I, too often, will say nothing to the contrary. Why? It lessens the blow of the dissonance. It keeps me sane.

In another conflicting sense, using she/her/hers pronouns also allows me to plunge deeper into the dissonance, to confuse the rigidity of my culture even more by refusing to "match" my non-binary identity with "non-binary pronouns." A person of any gender can assume any pronouns they wish; and in doing so myself, I feel empowered and further detached from the standards of my society.

While there is a lot of freedom in which pronouns people can use to express themselves, it's important to understand that pronouns can be a very serious and personal choice for many trans/nb folks. Please follow these best practices for respecting other people's pronouns:

- If you don't know someone's pronouns, try not to assume. Consider simply using their name, using gender neutral pronouns, or breaking the ice by introducing yourself with *your* pronouns first. *(Example: "Hi my name is Ash and I use she/her/ they/them pronouns. What name/pronouns do you go by?")*

- When someone informs you of their pronouns, say thank you and make an effort to use those words when describing that person.

- If you do mess up and use the wrong pronouns by mistake, acknowledge your mistake, apologize, and move on.

- Don't use pronouns as a weapon to poke fun at trans/non-binary folks. (*Example: "I identify as part toaster, part special snowflake. My pronouns are toast/toastself." It's not funny or cute to make fun of marginalized communities you're not a member of.*)

- Note that some feel that when cis people use non-traditional pronouns "just cause" or as leverage to include themselves in trans/nb conversations, it can dismiss the oppression trans/nb face with their pronouns. It is always important to be mindful of the privileges one has and remember that certain actions might trivialize others' experiences.[71]

At the end of the day, your pronouns might be important to you, or they might not be. They might express your gender, they might not. The major takeaway from this section is, as long as you're remaining respectful, use whatever pronouns you think are best for you. Pronouns are words meant to best represent the person they are referring to, and only that person can decide what the right way to do that is.

---

71. Being cis and using non-traditional pronouns "just cause" is different than doing so because you are questioning and/or experimenting. Questioning your identity and trying new things in order to learn more about yourself is always ok!

Likewise, never feel bad requesting that others use your chosen pronouns. You deserve respect and to be affirmed in your identity. Your feelings are totally valid, whatever you decide is right for you!

Part 2:

GENDER

CHAPTER 2:

Identities and Terms

Now that we've investigated the definitions of sex, gender, gender expression and pronouns, and we've deconstructed some of ways society views these concepts, let's plunge into the colossal ocean of colorful terminology and gender identities that exist!

Before we get into the nitty gritty stuff, I feel it's important to stress again that this book should not be used to label anyone in any way that makes them uncomfortable. Below I provide only *some* of the most common gender terms, identities and definitions. However, different people can self-identify with these words in different ways. A label doesn't define a person's identity. While some people might "fit the definition," they still may not use that label because it may not resonate with them. That is totally valid!

You may also notice that many labels have definitions that seem to overlap, which may seem confusing. There are many similar labels/terms/genders, but for some people there are important, often subtly nuanced, differences between each. You don't have to understand them all (there's no quiz), just know that different words exist because different people connect to them in different ways.

Finally, if you find yourself lost or confused at all while perusing this detailed list of terms, I want to offer a word of encouragement. You are doing good just by being curious and open to different identities. You don't have to become an expert of these terms by any means. Rather than memorize this list, simply keep it as a handy reference. Also, be sure to continue exploring your own identity, always with a freedom to move from label to label as you discover new things about yourself and find new definitions or ways of describing gender.

Cisgender/Cis: When a person is "cisgender" or "cis," this means **they identify exclusively with the gender/sex they were assigned at birth.** (*Example: My best friend Emily was assigned female at birth and identifies as a woman. She is a cisgender woman.*)

Man: A man is **someone who identifies as a man.** End of story.

Woman: A woman is **someone who identifies as a woman**. That's it.

Truth be told, the binary genders were probably the identities I've been most excited about defining this entire book. As we've established, "man" and "woman" are identities that have many unnecessary, anatomical and cultural expectations tied to them. In the end though, all it takes to be one of these genders, is to identify as such. It's time we start respecting and believing each others' individual experiences. If a person says they are a certain gender, we need to honor that. After all, these labels are all subjective. Who is to say one person's definition is more valid than another?

Speaking of binary genders and varying interpretations of labels, here is Chase to break down what being a man means to him.[72]

"Being a man" or "becoming a man" comes with many prerequisites and expectations in society. Men are told to act tough, be dominant, objectify women, and be masculine. But what is masculinity? Is it something only men can be a part of? Being a man has nothing to do with masculinity, being tough, being dominant, or even the genitals you were born with.

Being a man, for me, has always been about my personal comfort when navigating this world. When people use "he" when referring to me, it feels right. As a very feminine trans guy, I can attest to the societal expectations to act tough and "be a man" in order for the world to see me as who I really am.

This is part of a pattern that has been in society for years called "toxic masculinity." When individuals believe the only way to be a man is to follow "traditional" ideals of masculinity, this is where toxic masculinity comes into play and hurts the people it targets. The gender roles we are taught as children are a huge reason why toxic masculinity exists. When little boys are told to not "be a sissy" and to "man up," it gives the impression that being anything other than "masculine" is undesirable. Therefore, these individuals will grow up believing there is only one way to be a man.

---

72. Find more Chase here: http://bit.ly/2cb4KOg

But being a man has everything to do with listening to your body, understanding your feelings, and choosing how you navigate this world. Being a man to me is also standing up for people with less privilege and giving them space to shine and express themselves. Just remember that the notions most people have of masculinity are solely based on what they were taught; being a man is so much more than these stereotypes.

Now that we've covered some of the more widely recognized terms let's transition[73] and dive into some of the more mis- and underrepresented gender identities.

Transgender/Trans: This is an **umbrella term[74] for any person whose gender differs from the sex and/or gender they were assigned at birth.**

In order to better understand trans identities, let's explore some trans terminology.

Gender dysphoria: **Distress or unhappiness experienced because one's gender does not match their sex/gender assigned at birth.** There are two main types of dysphoria:

- Social: This kind of dysphoria is triggered by social situations. *(Example: The feeling when strangers automatically assume you to be a certain gender which you are not.)*

---

73. PUN!

74. Umbrella term: A word or phrase that collectively describes or refers to more than one identity/ orientation/group of people. Many of the umbrella terms in this book can also double as specific, or stand-alone identities. Umbrella terms are useful because they allow us to group, understand, and refer to a multitude of people while still allowing for ambiguity and autonomy.

- Body: This kind of dysphoria is related to one's body. It occurs when gender identity clashes with physical appearance. *(Example: The feeling a trans man might have when he hugs someone and is reminded that his chest is larger than he feels it should be.)*

Many of us may have heard of the narrative of the transgender person who felt "trapped in the wrong body." Some trans people legitimately do feel like this (and they are completely valid) however many trans people do not. Though that's the main narrative told in the media, it's far from the only one.[75]

The experience of dysphoria is different for every trans person. For some, dysphoria is a subtle nagging dissatisfaction, while for others it's an extreme, profound sorrow. What's more, there are also trans individuals who experience little to no dysphoria; it's not a requirement for being trans. Here is Milo to share his unique story with dysphoria.[76]

Discovering their dysphoria is a common way that transgender people figure out their transgender identities. It makes sense that they would realize they don't identify with their assigned genders by observing their discomfort with the part of their bodies that this assignment was based on. However, many trans people don't experience much (if any) dysphoria and must figure out their identity differently.

For example, I became aware of my gender through my experiences of gender euphoria, an emotion I feel when my gender is affirmed. I first experienced this when a child teased me for looking like a boy because I had short hair. Joke's on you, kiddo!

---

75. Riley made an excellent video on this topic: http://bit.ly/2c3fl2M
76. Find more Milo here: http://bit.ly/2c9CFbn

Even though I can describe specific experiences with my gender, some people will still say that I'm "not really trans" or that I'm "just a trans-trender" because I don't experience a lot of body dysphoria. Being told that I'm not transgender because I don't experience enough dysphoria is disheartening because people who tell me such usually assume I've had no real struggles as a transgender person.

I believe that all transgender people face some struggles because of their identity, but I don't believe that transgenderism should be defined in such a negative way (or in any way that is meant to be gatekeeping). After all, gender is not defined by one's genitals, so how could it be defined by what genitals one feels comfortable having? While my feminine voice doesn't make me dysphoric, being called "she" does have that effect on me.[77] But neither of those facts should open up my gender to public scrutiny.

Gender euphoria: **The feeling of extreme happiness, or comfort, because someone's gender is being affirmed.** Like Milo mentioned, gender euphoria is the counter to gender dysphoria. Like dysphoria this can also be triggered by social or physical situations. *(Example: The first time a trans woman puts on makeup and feels beautiful, or when a classmate begins utilizing the correct pronouns for their trans friend, making them feel affirmed.)*

---

77. An example of social dysphoria.

Transition: **The process of accepting oneself and/or pursuing changes in order to affirm one's gender and/or alleviate dysphoria.**[78] Often transitioning involves altering one's physical presentation, but it is not limited to this. Some of the ways people transition (among other things) are listed on the next page.

78. The "and/or" in "the process of accepting oneself *and/or* pursuing changes..." is very important. Like we've mentioned before, every trans person's experience is different. Some people may transition by *both* accepting themselves and pursuing outward changes (e.g. physical, name, pronoun changes, etc.), while others might only do one of these things. For some individuals, simply accepting themselves is all they need to do to feel they have transitioned. They may be happy with their body/name/pronouns/etc. and not have any desire to change those things. Some people may not use or identify with the word "transition" at all, even if they have done, are doing and/or intend to do any of the above things. What's more, someone may pursue physical/name/pronoun/etc. changes, but still struggle with accepting themselves. Self-acceptance is not required to transition or to start transitioning. In the end, the process of transitioning, if one even considers oneself to be transitioning at all, is a very unique and personal experience for everyone.

- Chest binding/genital tucking

- "Top surgery" (breast removal/augmentation)

- "Bottom surgery" (genital surgery)

- Hormones (hormone replacement therapy, "HRT")

- Switching pronouns

- Choosing a new name

- Changing the clothes one wears

- Getting a haircut/growing out one's hair

- Voice training

- Altering one's legal gender marker or name

- Allowing oneself to identify the way they feel is right

- Loving and accepting oneself as they are

- Cultivating pride in one's gender identity

- And more!

There is no "right" way to transition. Some trans people may pursue many of the things in this list, and some may pursue none of them. How a person presents, or expresses their gender, doesn't make their gender any more or less valid. Here is Ryan to explain how his gender expression is related to his identity.[79]

At age 16, I contemplated starting testosterone (T). I thought that with T, society would more readily accept me as a man, and my life would be easier. It was a big decision however and there were many obstacles in my way, so ultimately I decided to wait until I was older to start hormones.

Today, I'm really glad I decided to wait because by age 18 I no longer wanted to go on T. Do I sometimes want a beard and a more masculine body shape? Yes. But I don't want my singing voice to change and testosterone would definitely change my singing voice.

My lack of transitioning with testosterone didn't mean that I wasn't going to transition in other ways though. At age 18, I finally got top surgery and my chest dysphoria disappeared. Getting top surgery was something that I had to do for me. Testosterone was something that I wanted to do to please society. This helped me realize that I could only transition for

79. Find more Ryan here: http://bit.ly/2cmHtNL

myself. I had to follow the path that was right for me, not what was easier for the people around me. Today, I'm happy to be transgender and I'm happy that I followed my path. I accept myself for who I am and that is all that really matters.

As we mentioned earlier the word "transgender" can be an umbrella term. This means it can encompass many different identities within it. Next, let's explore some some of the identities that fall under the trans umbrella.

Trans man:[80] **Someone who was assigned female at birth and is a man.** A trans man may, or may not, choose to transition.

FTM: **Acronym for "female to male,"** a term sometimes used to refer to trans men.[81]

Transmasculine: A term used to **describe someone who was assigned female at birth, and who has a predominantly masculine gender and/or expresses themselves in a way they describe as masculine.** While transmasculine people feel a connection to masculinity, they may not identify in part or in whole as male. Transmasculine people can include:

- Trans men

- Demiguys[82]

- Non-binary people who consider themselves to be masculine

- Non-binary who feel their gender is more masculine than anything else

- Multigender people who feel more masculine than anything else[83]

- Genderfluid people who predominately feel masculine[84]

---

80. This term is sometimes alternatively spelled "transman." Some people dislike this spelling because they feel "trans" is an adjective. Like black man or queer man, it's a way of explaining the intersection of identities a person holds. They feel conjoining it with the word "man" implies that a "transman" is not a man the same way a "cis man" is. Others feel differently, and like to use "transman" as a single word. Some do this because they feel their transness is as much a part of their gender as their manhood is.
81. Some people are moving away from this term because it implies trans men were once female.
82. See page 104 for more on the term "demi."
83. See page 103 for more on the term "multigender."
84. See page 114 for more on the term "genderfluid."

Male to Male/MTM: **This is a person whose sex/gender was assigned female at birth and who rejects that their gender was ever female.** They have never felt a connection with a female gender and thus don't identify as FTM. Some MTM people who transition, use this term because it is not their *gender* that is transitioning but their *presentation*.

Trans woman:[85] **Someone who was assigned male at birth and is a woman.** A trans woman also may, or may not, choose to transition.

MTF: **Acronym for "male to female,"** a term sometimes used to refer to trans women.[86]

Transfeminine: A term used to **describe someone who was assigned male at birth, and who has a predominantly feminine gender and/or expresses themselves in a way they describe as feminine.** While transfeminine people feel a connection to femininity, they may not identify in part or in whole as female. Transfeminine people can include:

- Trans women

- Demigirls

- Non-binary people who consider themselves to be feminine.

- Non-binary people who feel their gender is more feminine than anything else

- Multigender people who feel more feminine than anything else

- Genderfluid people who predominately feel feminine

Female to Female/FTF: **This is a person whose sex/gender was assigned male at birth and who rejects that their gender was ever male.** They have never felt a connection with a male gender and thus don't identify as MTF. Some FTF people who transition,

---

85. This term is sometimes alternatively spelled "transwoman." Some people dislike this spelling because they feel "trans" is an adjective. Like black woman or queer woman, it's a way of explaining the intersection of identities a person holds. They feel conjoining it with the word "woman" implies that a "transwoman" is not a woman the same way a "cis woman" is. Others feel differently, and like to use transwoman as a single word. Some people, including Eli Erlick (one of the wonderful editors of this book), do this because they feel their transness is as much a part of their gender as their womanhood is.

86. Some people are moving away from this term because it implies trans women were once men.

use this term because it is not their *gender* that is transitioning but their *presentation*.

So far we have mainly covered trans identities that involve being a binary gender. However, it is important to acknowledge that trans identities are not limited to men and women. A person could also identify as trans and agender, trans and non-binary, trans and neutrois, trans and maverique, trans and bigender, trans and trigender, and etc.

Transsexual: This word has two common definitions:

- **A person whose gender is different from their sex/gender assigned at birth.** (Similar to transgender.)

- **A person who has undergone, or hopes to undergo, some kind of medical transition.**[87]

Don't refer to a person as a "transsexual" without their permission. Many are averse to using this term because:

- It's older and feels dated.

- It has a strong medical connotation.

- It has history of being used in ignorant, derogatory ways.

DFAB/AFAB/FAAB: These are acronyms for **"designated female at birth," "assigned female at birth,"** and **"female assigned at birth."**

DMAB/AMAB/MAAB: These are acronyms for **"designated male at birth," "assigned male at birth,"** and **"male assigned at birth."**

The above terms are used by non-cis people who wish to communicate what gender/sex they were perceived as and labeled at birth. This phrase was created to stress that the gender/sex in question was assigned by society and isn't a reflection of their actual gender. These are the terms that should be used as opposed to the grossly inaccurate and insensitive alternative of, "the gender someone was born as." The latter implies that anyone, cis or not, was

---

87. Undergoing a medical transition does not mean a person is required to identify as a transsexual. Also, it's important to note that medically transitioning does not make someone "more trans" or more legitimate than a trans person who does not medically transition. There is no trans hierarchy or "best way" to be trans.

born into a particular category of gender rather than said category being assigned by a doctor at birth, thus in turn implying that a trans woman, for example, wasn't born a woman.

A similar, but still slightly different term from DFAB/AFAB/FAAB and DMAB/AMAB/MAAB is...

CAFAB/CAMAB: These are acronyms for **"coercively assigned female/male at birth."** The biggest difference between these terms and the previous terms is obviously the addition of the word "coercively." This was added to emphasize the lack of agency and forceful, coercive nature of sex/gender assignment.

There was a time when these terms were very contentious. Some people felt they should only be used by intersex people because many intersex people are forced to undergo invasive and nonconsensual surgeries. After all, while trans/nb people's genders are unrightfully dictated, the process is more designational or decisional, a doctor checking off a box rather than altering genitals. Thus, some felt the word "coercively" reflected intersex people's experiences more accurately than trans/nb people's.

Others argued this was unfair because trans people coined the terms, and while they may not endure unconsented surgeries, their sex/gender assignment is still coercive.

Over time there seemed to be a consensus reached that intersex people, trans people, nb people, and anyone non-cis can all share these terms, and rightfully use these terms to describe themselves if they choose.

It is undeniable however, that intersex people and trans/nb people undergo very different forms of oppression. This why some people feel intersex individuals should have their own terms to describe their unique experience if they wish. This led to the coinage of the terms...

IAFAB/IAMAB and FAFAB/FAMAB: Acronyms for **"intersex assigned female/male at birth"** and **"forcibly assigned female/male at birth."**

Intersex people certainly do not have to identify with these terms, but they can if they choose (as it is with any person and any label!).

What's more, these terms are exclusively reserved for intersex individuals. Use by anyone else would be appropriative.

Bigender: **Someone who has/experiences two genders.**

- These genders can be binary or non-binary.

- A person can experience both genders simultaneously or alternate between them.

- A person does not have to experience each gender equally and/ or in the same way.

(Example: Someone who is bigender might be both a man and woman, non-binary and a woman, or agender and neutrois.)

Here is Axel to tell you about what being bigender is like for them.[88]

Hi my names Axel, and I'm bigender. This means that some days I'm male, other days I'm female, and sometimes I'm both. I'm 85% male, 10% female, and that other 5% is both. I mostly present as male because that's what makes me more comfortable.

To better understand and be comfortable with my gender, I've been seeing a transgender therapist. She's helped me figure out how I want to move forward. We've discussed whether or not I wanted to start hormones and/ or have top surgery. She's also helped me understand a lot of the fears I have. I've now come to terms with the fact that; yes, I was born a girl, but for the most part I'm a guy.

---

88. Find more of Axel here: http://bit.ly/2cHr1Hk

I have decided the best thing for me is to start hormone treatment in the next few months and eventually get top surgery. I'm glad that people will get to see the guy that I see in my head almost every day. Yes, my female side is still there, but in the long run I realized this will make me the happiest. Which is what I wish for everyone in the transgender community; happiness, love, and just being comfortable with yourself.

Trigender: **Someone who has/experiences three genders.**

- These genders can be binary or non-binary.

- A person can experience all three genders simultaneously or alternate between them.

- A person does not have to experience each gender equally and/ or in the same way.

Multigender/Polygender: **Someone who has/experiences more than one gender.** A person may choose to identify with this because the number of genders they have/experience is unknown or fluctuates.

Pangender/omnigender: Many pangender or omnigender people recognize that our current knowledge of gender is limited. They believe that genders exist which we do not yet know about, and that there could possibly be an infinite amount of genders. **Pan/ Omnigender people experience many, and sometimes, all of these genders.** These multigender experiences can occur simultaneously, or once at a time.

Some important things to note about these terms:

- Some people see these labels as potentially problematic. Many are skeptical regarding how someone could experience or have *all* genders.

- Also, there's the fact that some genders are intrinsically linked to specific cultures and societies. Thus, if you are not a member of said cultures or societies, claiming an identity that belonged to them would be appropriative.

As a result of these potential problems, the following label was created...

Maxigender: **Maxigender people experience many, and sometimes, all available genders to them.**

- This term is different from the aforementioned labels because it actively acknowledges that certain genders are linked to specific cultures and societies. Maxigender only includes genders that are available (i.e. that would not be appropriative to claim) for that person. *(Example: It would be appropriative for someone who isn't Indian or Native American to claim an identity like Hijira or Two Spirit[89] as these identities are explicitly tied to the aforementioned cultures. Maxigender recognizes this and does not include those genders for people not a part of those cultures.)*

Demi-: **Someone who has/experiences a partial connection to the gender(s) in question.** *(Example usages: demiguy, demiboy, demigirl, deminon-binary, demifluid, demiagender)*

I, for instance identify with this term. Let me elaborate.

I feel ...kinda like a girl, but also ...kinda not. A moment that comes to mind which illustrates these feelings, happened once at party.

It was a co-ed, college party, that my friends decided should have a ritzy, old timey, gambling theme. Before everyone arrived, many of the gals attending gathered in the basement of our house to get ready together. There were cosmetics and curling irons galore. After only a couple hours, every woman had managed to transform themselves into either a sexy

---

89. As I claim neither of these identities and was not able to successfully contact people who do, they are not defined in this book. Feel free to research them on your own if you wish to learn more!

flapper or a glamorous showgirl. So when I stepped upstairs wearing a vest, pants, and a tie, a small coup arose.

"A tie?"

"You can't wear that!"

And then, a phrase that evoked both strong and confusing emotions within me,

"Of course she can, it's Ashley, she's not like, a REAL girl."

Although I knew my friend's intention was to lighten the mood, and stand up for my right to wear what I like, it immediately flipped a defensive switch within me. My mind raced through a lengthy, internal monologue that went something like,

"I most certainly am a girl! Perhaps not in the way society expects, but growing up as a woman has shaped who I am. It's made me powerful, thoughtful, and compassionate. If you stripped that title from me, I wouldn't feel complete. I am a woman!"

Quickly, another friend chimed in before my inner thoughts could continue their silent ranting,

"Psh, Ashley is too a girl, shut up Kate."

Surprisingly, my guttural reaction to that sentiment however was,

"No I'm not."

It was the most confused, wishy-washy, internal defense and explanation of my identity I had ever experienced. On one hand, I most definitely felt like a woman. While on the other hand, I absolutely did not. How could this be?

After a few days of reflection, I decided the answer to this question was, because I am a woman who also has some very agender and fluid elements to their identity. Apparently, it's very important that all these aspects are acknowledged when I'm being labeled. That's why the word "woman" on its own, doesn't feel quite right. This is also why I feel a connection to the word demigirl.

Aporagender: **Both a specific gender identity and an umbrella term for being a non-binary gender separate from man, woman, and anything in between while still having a very strong and specific gendered feeling.**

Maverique: Someone who has an **autonomous gender which exists entirely independent of the binary genders man and woman.** If genders were colors, a maverique's gender would be yellow; a primary color that is in no way derived from any other colors.

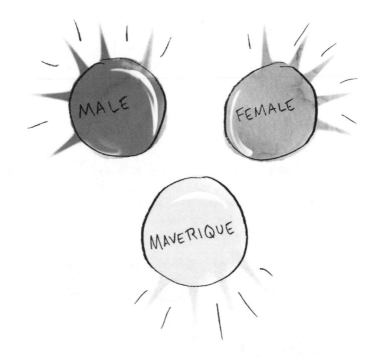

Both aporagender and maverique were coined at almost exactly the same time by different people, and while they do share some similarity, they are each their own distinct identity. Aside from each identity having its own distinct community, the biggest difference between them is that one can be used as an umbrella term to refer to various genders (aporagender) while the other is specifically a distinct gender of its own (maverique).

Despite these distinctions, sometimes choosing to use one word over another to describe one's gender can also be a matter of personal preference. Some people even identify as both aporagender and maverique simultaneous, just as some people identify as both bi and pan.[90]

Vesper, one of the fantastic editors of this book and coiner of the term, explains what maverique means to them on the next page.[91]

90. See pages 145–149 for more on bi and pan.
91. Find more Vesper here: http://bit.ly/1Pm404S

Knowing that I was neither male nor female, while at the same time also not being somewhere in between those binary genders nor genderless, I first referred to my non-binary gender as "neutrois." Conceptualizing my gender when seemingly all genders, even non-binary ones, derive from/trace back to the two binary genders in some way (be it being a combination of them, fluctuating in between them or being only partially connected to them) was extremely hard. I knew that my gender had nothing whatsoever to do with those two genders, but also that I definitely was not genderless either.

Because of this strong sense of my own gender and the subsequent strong disconnect that I felt even with other non-binary genders, I felt isolated and alone even among other non-binary people. There wasn't a single word with which to communicate the gender I felt to others, but I eventually settled on neutrois because "neither" or "gender neutral" was as best as it seemed I could do in approximating the gender that I felt.

However, in the two years that I spent identifying as neutrois, the term never felt right either. This is because "neither" was still incredibly vague while my actual gender was not vague at all and "gender neutral" still implied some sort of connection to or commentary on the gender binary, which I felt zero tie to. I continued to feel dismayed.

Out of sheer exasperation and desperation, I decided to take matters into my own hands and coin my own word to describe the gender that I've felt my entire life. That word was "maverique," franglais that is a combination of the English eponym "maverick" and the French suffix "-ique."

In coining maverique I not only equipped myself with the ability to communicate who I am to other people, I also helped equip others with that same ability, which in turn has helped maveriques in general be able to find and communicate with each other. As someone who felt marooned on my own tiny island of gender for so long, having this newfound community of maveriques around me was, and continues to be incredible beyond words.

Far too often people underestimate the power a word and a sense of identity can have, but this maverique learned that firsthand. I will forever stand tall and be proud of who I am, both as a non-binary person but especially as a maverique.

Non-binary: **Both a specific identity and an umbrella term for gender identities outside the gender binary.** A non-binary person could be neither man nor woman, multiple genders simultaneously, flowing between genders, or something entirely different.

Identifying as non-binary is a unique experience, and here is KB to tell us more about it.[92]

When I grew up there were no words for non-binary identities, you were one thing: boy or girl. Anything in between that was just a personal trait you had, like how tomboys were boyish and boys could be girlish. For most of my life I identified as my birth assignment.

Non-binary for me is something I personally had to discover. It wasn't put on a plate for me to eat, and it wasn't an answer to a hard question. Non-binary is an extension of who I am. It doesn't define my interactions, my feelings, or what I do on Saturdays. It's just a feeling. It's like how when I finally got glasses and noticed that the stars flickered or that the moon had shadows. Things that were there this whole time, but I've only just realized.

---

92. Find more KB here: http://bit.ly/2bWq8pt

I consider non-binary to be less of an expression of gender(s) and more of a explanation. I kept searching for something that made me feel like myself. I was never just one thing and now that I can identify with an identity that can regard multiple things, bigender, agender etc. I now have a word that can help people understand that I'm not just two boxes with a check mark inside the one that matches my genitals. I identify with non-binary and yet I'm sure I haven't figured everything out about it, but that's okay.

I still go by my birth pronouns in real life, and I still use my assigned gender. The only difference is now I have a word for what I am. For me personally, non-binary is a word that helps me understand me just a little bit more.

Nb: This is an **abbreviation/nickname/shorthand form of non-binary.**

Enby: **This is slang term meaning "a non-binary person."** It comes from the pronunciation of "nb." (*Example usage: "Enbies are amazing people!"*)

Genderqueer: **Someone whose gender exists outside of or beyond society's binary concept of gender, often by not conforming to it.** Genderqueer is both a specific identity and an umbrella term that describes a multitude of non-normative gender identities, people, expressions, etc.

Gender Nonconforming/Gender Diverse/Gender Variant/Gender-Expansive:[93] **These are also umbrella terms which refer to people who identify and/or express themselves in ways that are different from society's binary norms.**

The key distinctions between these terms and "genderqueer" is that while these words can be identities, they are more commonly used as descriptors (for a specific person, groups of people, clothing, expression, behavior, etc.)

These terms can also relate to both cis and non-cis people. (*Example: Someone who is non-binary could be considered gender nonconforming as their very gender is nonconformative. Additionally, a cis woman who describes her style as "tomboyish" could also be considered gender nonconforming as her style would be nonconformative.*)

Here is Cady to tell us what being gender nonconforming is like for them.[94]

To me, gender nonconforming means not adhering to either of the binary genders, whether that be by expression, behavior, identity or all of the aforementioned. As a non-binary person, I identify as gender nonconforming because I don't feel I have a gender at all. Thus, however I act, behave or dress is gender nonconforming because it's me doing those things.

---

93. Gender variant is falling out of favor however because it establishes cisgender as the norm that is varied from.
94. Find more Cady here: http://bit.ly/2cmGNrO

Although gender and gender expression are not inherently linked, I feel most comfortable dressing in an androgynous manner. This contributes to my appearance sometimes confusing strangers, who are unable to immediately place me into a male or female box. In such a binary-orientated world, it's very comforting to be able to communicate with other gender nonconforming people; representation and feeling a sense of belonging within a community is so important.

Having support and acceptance from others, as well as from myself, allows me to look past arbitrarily gendered things like bathrooms and instead look good wearing my binder, vibrantly painted nails and a pair of really nice patterned socks.

Gender Confusion/Gender F*ck: **A person who deliberately seeks to cause, or enjoys when they create, confusion in regards to their own gender.**

You might be thinking to yourself, why would anyone want to confuse people about their gender? Well, there are several reasons:

- To make a statement about gender norms and roles.

- To inspire discussion surrounding gender issues.

- Because they are comfortable existing in ambiguous or androgynous spaces.

Listen to Kai's experiences to hear from someone who identifies as a gender confusion first hand.[95]

One of my most vivid memories from primary school is the time a classmate came forward about being completely confused by me and my gender. If I remember correctly, she asked me if I was a boy dressed up as a girl in order to go to school there. (I went to an all-female school.) As a ten-year-old, that question made me exceptionally happy and thinking back to it today still makes me smile.

There could've been any number of reasons for her to ask me that — I was never one to gossip or sit in a circle painting my nails and I could often be found climbing trees or talking about "masculine" sports and hobbies. However, the day she asked me happened to be a casual clothes day and in my usual style of masculine and feminine mixture, I must have appeared to be very masculine.

---

95. Find more Kai here: http://bit.ly/2ce1wco

That was the first time anyone expressed confusion towards my gender, and I've been searching for it ever since. I live in South Africa where non-binary genders seem to still be a myth or a scary story told around a campfire. This makes gender nonconforming a bit more difficult, but I still relish the moments when someone refers to me as "sir - uh - madam? Sorry."

Maybe it's my love of challenging the gender binary or maybe it's my desire to heal the closed-mindedness of my fellow South Africans, but identifying as a gender confusion has always given me joy and I doubt I'm going to stop anytime soon.

Genderfluid: **Having a gender that changes.** A genderfluid person's identity can fluctuate between genders, and/or they can experience multiple genders simultaneously. Their identity may shift totally at random and/or based on circumstance.

My friend Roland has recently come out as genderfluid. This is how they came to realize their identity.[96]

Being genderfluid has been one of the most confusing yet liberating things I've experienced. This is partly because, trying to differentiate between my gender expression and identity was hard! As someone who "looks

---

96. Find more Roland here: http://bit.ly/2cJKKHz

like a man" regardless of what I wear or do, I've been told so many times that I'm just a gay boy who likes to express himself in a girly way. I was told that this had nothing to do with my gender. I also grew up in a place where if a person crosses the line into gender bending they can get abuse openly thrown at them in the streets. This caused me to suppress all my gender-related feelings.

Last summer though, I moved to London with my YouTube friends and I was able to dress in girls clothes and experiment with makeup completely free from judgement. It was the most eye opening experience! I was so used to being told what I could and could not wear and do; I almost forgot what real happiness felt like. I was still trying to work out my exact identity though. My feelings seemed to change day to day and no one could give me a definitive answer to what I felt inside.

So I searched for different genders online and came across "genderfluid." BAM! It was like fireworks going off in my head. YES! This is you. This is how you feel. After being so confused for so long, finally understanding myself was like being on a euphoric high!

Fast forward to now, and I realize that moving away was the best thing I could have done! I had no idea how unhappy I was back in my hometown and how much it was holding me back inside. Understanding my gender and not letting it determine anything I do, is the most freeing feeling I've ever had. I want people to know you don't need to look a certain way to identify as a non-binary gender.

Genderflux: **Someone whose experience with gender changes (fluctuates) in intensity.** *(Example: a genderflux person may feel intensely or distinctly like a man sometimes, but at other times they may feel only slightly or somewhat like a man.)*

This identity can be tricky to fully understand, so here is my friend Isabel to help explain what being genderflux means to them.[97]

When I first started to question my gender, I had seen people like Ruby Rose explaining that they were genderfluid. At first, I thought, that's me! My whole life I'd never really thought about my gender at all, and as I'm dfab, I had just kind of accepted I was a tomboy as a kid and then "grew up". Yet, I realised there were only a few distinct times I remember feeling feminine (something I later discovered most girls felt frequently), and started to wonder what I felt like the rest of the time.

I quickly decided I wasn't genderfluid, as I learnt that is most commonly a shift between genders, like two different sides of the same coin (although I'm sure this analogy doesn't suit everyone!).

Yet for me, I felt like I had all these different parts and feelings in me at once, which were more dominant on certain days, barely traceable on others, and always changing subtlety.

---

97. Find more Isabel here: http://bit.ly/2bXICuN

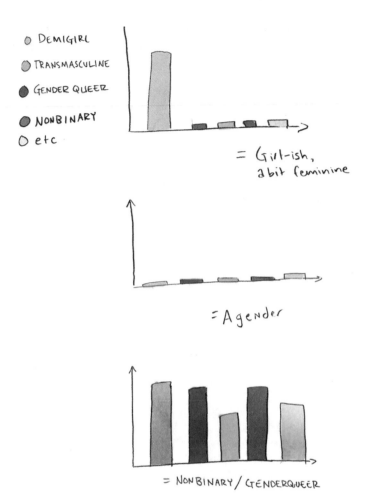

○ DEMIGIRL
◔ TRANSMASCULINE
● GENDER QUEER
● NONBINARY
○ etc

= Girl-ish,
a bit feminine

= Agender

= NONBINARY / GENDERQUEER

I began to think about my gender as a column graph. For me, the bars include, demigirl, transmasculine, genderqueer, non-binary, and a whole lot of other things I can feel like. If the demigirl bar is up one day and the others are down, I will feel kinda girl-ish and a bit feminine. Some days I feel like a few of the bars are high, and I might just ID as non-binary, genderqueer, or androgyne[98] for the day depending on what I feel best suits that combination of present feelings or genders. Yet if all the bars are down low, I won't feel anything, and go by agender.

---

98. See page 120 for more on "androgyne."

While I am poly-genderflux (meaning I experience several different genders fluctuating), genderflux to others could just be some days feeling like a boy, and then other days not really having the same vibe.

Essentially to me, genderflux describes the increase, decrease, and changing of my connection to and with a gender. When more than one gender fluctuates, these feelings can combine and interact, and create even more possibilities and ways to experience my gender.

Androgynous: **Possessing qualities that are both masculine and feminine, neither masculine nor feminine, and/or in between masculinity and femininity.**

The evolution of the term androgynous is an interesting one. The term's original definition solely involved possessing *both* masculine and feminine qualities. It wasn't until later that young people started adopting "androgynous" to mean "neither masculine nor feminine" or "in between masculine and feminine."

Some people find this shift frustrating because they feel it erases the word's original definition. After all, when asked to picture an androgynous person, most people today would probably say that "a gender ambiguous kid in skinny jeans with an undercut" comes to mind before "someone both wearing a dress and rocking a buzzcut."

Knowing how to handle this shift in androgyny's meaning is tricky. Ideally we would remember and recognize the word's original definition, while simultaneously embracing the word's new users and meaning. This, in my opinion, is the best way to neither erase identities, nor police them.

The concept of androgyny can be applied to many things: gender, fashion, interests, sexual identity, behavior, physical features, names and so on. The term can relate to cis people as well as non-cis people.

Ky is a fabulous youtuber here to tell you about what androgyny means to him...and probably make you jealous of his contouring skills.[99]

Hey there, I'm Ky! I'm just your ordinary 19-year-old boy. What makes me ordinary, you may ask? Well for starters, in high school I enjoyed

---

99. Find more Ky here: http://bit.ly/2cb5eEc

playing many sports. I almost went to state on my high schools wrestling team even! I also liked playing video games and going camping with the boy scouts, and as a young teen I thought it was fun to put on makeup and dress in wigs for funny videos!

Oh wait. I know what you're thinking — most guys don't wear wigs, and they probably don't know what the term "contour" means...How could I have been so different? I felt so out of place. No one understood me. I was too girly for the guys and too boyish for the girls.

Over time I started to embrace myself more. I did my makeup on the days I was feeling hella fabulous and other days I didn't care for makeup at all. It made me feel good to know I could express myself however I felt was right that day. Then a friend showed me a video of a man who taught male makeup tutorials and I was so intrigued! After a lot of research, I came across the word "androgyny."

The definition matched my identity so well! It showed me that I could wear clothes with a more fluid style. It also helped me realize I could show both my masculine and feminine characteristics! Now, instead of feeling alone and misunderstood like I did in the past, I know many other amazing people online who understand my identity. A few of them even identify as androgynous just like me!

So I was wrong, I was never alone! It just took some time for me to find myself, and once I did I found the people I would grow to share my identity with!

A similar, but slightly different term for androgynous is androgyne. The biggest distinction between these terms is that "androgynous" is more commonly used as a descriptor (to describe gender, expression, style, behavior, etc.) while "androgyne" is a specific identity/gender. Let's unpack this term some more.

Androgyne: This is a non-binary gender related to androgyny. **A person who identifies as an androgyne may identify as both a man and woman, neither a man nor woman, and/or somewhere in between man and woman.**

Joy identifies with the word androgyne and she shares an adorable, whimsical story which illustrates what the experience is like for her below.[100]

"So, androgyne? What is that? How do you even pronounce it? It looks like a fancy, foreign version of 'androgynous.' Is it different? I have no idea. Help!"

This was the internal dialogue that I experienced when I first came across the term in my quest to discover my gender identity, so if a similar something went through your mind too, here's an extremely metaphorical story to try and explain the why and how I identify with it.

100. Find more Joy here: http://bit.ly/2cxCzJY

Once upon a time, there was a princess. All of her life the king and queen told her that princesses behaved like ladies, wore beautiful dresses, trained in proper manners and elegance, and were to always wait for a handsome prince to come and save them if ever needed. Princes behaved like gentlemen, wore the finest suites, trained in swordsmanship and sailing, and were always ready to save a princess. This was the perfect formula for a "happily ever after," or at least that's what her parents always told her. What if they were wrong? Could her "happily ever after" look different?

One day, this particular human found herself to be in a bit of a pickle. She somehow ended up in the den of a vicious, multi-headed, fire-breathing dragon. She was not about to wait around for a prince to save her, partly because she didn't have time, and partly because she didn't need a prince. She had no sword, no shield, and no idea what to do. The dragon was closing in fast. Everything her parents had ever said to her reared their heads and spewed their awful fire in her face until she fell to the ground, burned and battered. She closed her eyes and wished with all of her heart that she had something to fight with.

Then, her fairy godmother, who had heard her desperate pleas, appeared in the nick of time with a shining suit of armor. She put on the armor and she kicked that dragon's ugly, judgmental ass!

In that moment, and for the rest of her life, she wasn't a princess and she wasn't a prince. She was a knight in shining armor: unidentifiable, strong, inimitable, and whole. She behaved with nobility, wore the most impenetrable armor, wielded her weapon with strength, trained her brain and her body, and never ever waited to be saved. She could slay dragons and go to afternoon tea with the queen in the same day. She could marry a princess. She was herself, and she lived happily ever after.

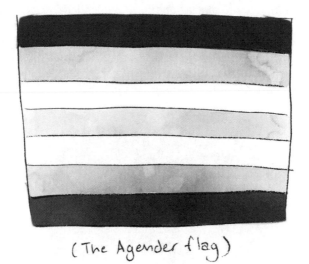

(The Agender flag)

Agender/genderless:[101] These labels can be interpreted in a few ways,

- The words themselves literally translate to **"without gender,"** and this is how some agender/genderless people feel, that they lack gender.

- Others who identify this way feel they are more **gender neutral.**

- Other people identify this way because **they reject the concept of gender entirely or think it is irrelevant for them personally.**

Chandler is agender and tells us what it's like for them below.[102]

Being agender can be a whirlwind of confusion when first coming out. It's like being uncomfortable with how the world sees you 99% of the time. This stems from the binary mindset that the majority of society is stuck in. Society tries to categorize people as either a man or a woman, so for those who are neither, it can make us feel tense.

---

101. Other words similar to agender include: genderblank, genderfree, null gender, non-gendered, no gender, and gender void. Some people use these words interchangeably; other people identify subtle, but important differences between them.
102. Find more Chandler here: http://bit.ly/2bXKB1S

I struggled coming to the conclusion that I'm agender and not a trans man because of this binary mindset. I was excited when people in public read me as a man, but then it occurred to me... it wasn't that I liked being seen as a man, it was that I liked not being seen as a woman. I didn't actually feel like a man though, and once I realized that, I could finally accept myself wholeheartedly as the agender person I am!

Some people know they're transgender from a very young age, but not me. I didn't realize I was agender until I was 16 years old. That's when it finally dawned on me that "she/her" pronouns were extremely uncomfortable and "he/him" pronouns weren't quite right either. It's one of those situations where you just have to go with what feels right, and for me, "they/them" pronouns made me very happy, helped me to feel comfortable, and accurately reflected my gender neutral identity. Once I had completely accepted myself, it was easier to let my self-conscious walls down and just really be true to myself.

Gender Neutral: **Having a gender that is neutral.** This can mean a couple of things:

- Feeling one's gender lands in the middle of the binary spectrum.

- Feeling one's gender has NOTHING to do with either of the binary genders.

Kaitlyn is a dope person who is constantly working on amazing web shows that all have wonderful LGBTQIA+ themes. They identify with the former version of this definition. Here is their story.[103]

When I was a kid, I always wore boy's clothes, played with girl's toys and hung out with everyone on the playground. I was a mishmash of gender, and I never felt comfortable with it. I remember I always felt like I was in this weird middle ground between genders. People would call me "her" and it would feel weird, but when people mistook me for a boy and called me "he" it felt just as weird. I honestly thought I was broken or something.

Two years ago, I got the role of a character named LaFontaine in a web series called "Carmilla" who identified as genderqueer and it kind of changed my perspective on everything. I wanted to do research to make sure I was representing a group of people properly, and in that research I stumbled upon the identity "gender neutral" and everything immediately clicked. I didn't have the education growing up to tell me that there were genders beyond male/female, so discovering that there was a term for what I felt was such a relief.

I now use the terms non-binary/gender neutral to describe myself, and I've been out for over a year now. So, to me, gender neutral just described how I felt: in the neutral ground between male/female and quite comfortable there.

Neutrois: **Someone who is neutrois may feel their gender is neutral or null.** A neutrois person may feel one of these things, switch between them, or identify with both of them at the same time.

This identity has a history of including people who experience dysphoria and/or wish to transition. Often people who feel this way prefer to remove any masculine/feminine gender indicators in order to make their appearance match their gender identity. This typically involves presenting in a very gender neutral or androgynous way. Some neutrois people also medically transition.

Experiencing dysphoria and/or transitioning is certainly not a requirement for being neutrois though. Many people who are neutrois experience little to no dysphoria and do not desire any kind of transition.

103. Find more Kaitlyn here: http://bit.ly/2cdQoic

Here is Jennifer's experience being neutrois.[104]

Being neutrois is living completely outside the gender binary. For me, neutrois is a gender identity exactly in the middle of the spectrum, but without any female- or maleness within it. I feel I do have a gender – I have a connection to a specific sense of self – and so do not relate with those that are genderless. It is this other gender (one that is not defined by body parts or expression nearly as much as the binary genders) that I feel a close connection with.

Because of my neutrois identity, I am honored by they/them/their pronouns, and prefer to be referred to with gender-neutral words such as "person" and "sibling". This actively shows recognition of my gender identity, but also leaves it ambiguous to those that aren't close friends, as gender is a very personal and private experience for me.

Very few people correctly use my pronouns, despite the fact they've been informed. This contributes to my gender dysphoria. I mainly experience social dysphoria, and have felt uncomfortable being grouped with others of a binary gender. It is this active misgendering that reinforces this "other" sense of self I have.

Let's circle back and address the relationship between the identities agender, genderless, gender neutral, and neutrois. Some may feel these terms are rather similar. So much so they may use these words interchangeably, identify with all of them, and/or find it hard to draw concrete lines distinguishing them from each other.

---

104. Find more Jennifer here: http://bit.ly/2c3gCqQ

Others may feel these identities are in fact very different. Often the differences between similar terms like these are subtle, but this doesn't mean they aren't *important* to those who identify with them. Slight distinctions and utilizing the correct identifier can really matter to certain people. The right label can provide a very specific description of a person's identity, which no other word may seem to have captured. It may not be until someone finds that word, or someone who uses it, that they see themselves for the first time, or have a word to describe their gender/orientation/etc.

Also, note that identities can be much more than a single word and its definition(s). Often there is history, community and various other things tied to an identity and that can also play a part in the overlap but subtle differences between identities and why a person may choose to identify (or disidentify) as something.

All the aforementioned situations and/or feelings are completely valid. Labels can be very powerful, and in the end, it's really up to the individual regarding which terms they adopt and how they define them. So yes, certain terms, definitions, and the differences between them might feel a bit ambiguous. This isn't a bad thing though as it allows for freedom and self-identification.[105]

Intergender: **A person who is intergender identifies between or as a mix of the binary genders, man and woman.** There is currently a debate concerning who can appropriately use this term. There are two primary schools of thought on this term:

1. It is a term for anyone to use who feels a connection with it.

2. It is a term that should only be used by intersex individuals. Anything otherwise would be appropriation. This is because there should be words for intersex individuals that reflect with their intersex identity. Non-intersex people should respect this and thus utilize different labels.

Gender Indifferent: **Being gender indifferent means being apathetic about one's gender/gender expression.** A person who is gender indifferent might not have any strong feeling about their personal gender or the concept of gender in general.

---

105. See the cheat sheet for more on "self identification."

Marion identifies as gender indifferent and describes what this means to them below.[106]

Immediately after realizing that I was "definitely not cis" during my junior year of high school, I started searching for a gender label that felt right. Honestly, I hated this process; I went through so many different labels. Some would feel great for a few days and others would only feel right for an hour. Even though I knew I didn't have to label my gender, I wanted to. This back and forth continued for three or four months before I found myself scrolling through Tumblr (the usual), and clicked on someone's blog. Their sidebar said that they ID'd as "gender indifferent", and though I have no memory of anything else about their blog, their label fit into my brain like puzzle pieces.

I'm gender indifferent and to me, it means being distanced from and apathetic towards my gender identity. Other than acknowledging and respecting the fact that I'm not cis, I feel "meh" *shrugs* about my gender; it doesn't have an impact on me. This sort of apathy reflects itself on my pronoun preferences (in my case they are preferences) and gender expression. As long as people know and understand that I am non-binary, it doesn't bother me what pronouns they use (when introducing myself I usually default to they/them to avoid assumptions). And, regarding my expression, I don't feel the need to physically manifest in a certain way, I wear what I like and what is comfortable based on my activities for that day.

It's been a weird road to finding a label that fits (and honestly, some days even this one feels a little off), but I'm glad to have found something a little more than "frantically searching for a label" to describe my non-binary-ness.

Graygender: **This identity involves having a weak sense of gender or being somewhat apathetic about one's gender identity/ expression/etc.** While graygender people *do* feel they have a gender, they may also feel:

- Disconnected from their gender

- Not overly involved in gender as a concept

- Not particularly invested in their gender

---

106. Find more Marion here: http://bit.ly/2cJLLiV

- That their gender is very intermittent

- That their gender is difficult to define

That brings us to the end of this section. Because the amount of genders that exist is endless, this book only skimmed the surface of gender education. Hopefully you have broadened your knowledge to some degree, and possibly even found a label or two you are excited to claim for yourself! If you're still on a hunt for your gender term after finishing this chapter, be sure to check out the other resources cited in the intro and throughout the book. These sites are bursting with further gender information, and if you still can't find your word after that, consider coining a new one!

Also, before you press forward, consider taking some time to reflect on your own gender by answering the following questions:

- Which gender(s) do you experience (if any)?

- How intensely do you experience your gender(s)? If you have more than one gender, do you experience your genders equally, or are some more intense than others?

- How often/intensely does your gender(s) change?

- Are you currently questioning anything about your gender?

- Are there words we've covered that you think might match/describe your gender?

Part 3:

SEXUAL AND ROMANTIC IDENTITIES

CHAPTER 3:

Sexual and Romantic Orientations: What Are They?

Now that we've tackled gender, gender identity, gender expression, and more, let's talk about what it means to be attracted to some (or none) of these things. The rest of this book will be devoted to unpacking some of the lesser known and commonly misunderstood sexual and romantic identities. Before we get into specifics though, let's define what "sexual orientation" and "romantic orientation" mean.

Sexual orientation:

A person's **sexual orientation** indicates who someone is/isn't sexually attracted to. This can include:

· What gender(s) they are sexually attracted to *(Example: "Only guys turn me on.")*

· How intensely/often they experience sexual attraction, if they even experience it at all *(Example: "I don't think I ever experience sexual attraction.")*

· How intensely/often their sexual attractions change/fluctuate *(Example: "Some days I only dig ladies but other days I find all genders sexy.")*

· The conditions under which they experience sexual attraction *(Example: "I can only be sexually attracted to someone after I form an emotional bond with them.")*

Sexual attraction can be defined as having a heightened interest in someone because they stimulate sexual desire or arousal. When and how this experience occurs is different from person to person because we all have different preferences, and also what is considered "sexual" is *subjective.*

For instance, kissing, for me, is incredibly sexual. A good kiss gives me goosebumps up and down, amps up my heart-rate, and makes me want to do the sexy things. This isn't the case for everyone, however. In fact, my friend Estelle views kissing very differently. Here are her thoughts on smoochin'.[107]

---

107. Find more Estelle here: http://bit.ly/2cdQciL

When I came out to a friend as asexual a couple years ago, one of the first things they asked me was, "So what about things like kissing?" And I, bewildered, answered in a stating-the-obvious tone: "......Kissing isn't sexual."

Since these kinds of things [sex/sexuality] often go undiscussed, I unconsciously took my opinion as the default, assuming everyone felt the same way. But you know what? Different gestures mean different things to different people! I've seen family members kiss each other on the mouth, acquaintances kiss each other on the cheek, and for my friend, it was hard for them to think of kissing as anything but sexual.

Personally, I have a lot of affection to give! And for me, kissing is one of many ways to do that. I give kisses to friends I love dearly, mostly on the cheek. And when it comes to romantic partners, making out is the greatest. But I've never felt a connection between kissing and sex. Hell, if I'm kissing someone with zero distance between us, it's still a nonsexual act on my end. For me, the wonderful wonders of kissing are purely platonic, romantic, or, at the very most, sensual."[108]

---

108. See page 139 for more on sensual and platonic attraction!

Now, if you're unsure whether or not you experience sexual attraction, don't panic; you're not alone. Many people who feel this way identify on the asexual spectrum.[109] This typically means the amount of sexual attraction they feel towards others can range from some, to little, to none, and/or fluctuate between amounts of attraction.

If you're curious, about how non-asexual people describe the experience of sexual attraction, a few common[110] characterizations of the experience include:

- Wanting to kiss someone

- Wanting to have sex with someone

- Finding your heart rate increase around someone

- Fantasizing about being sexual with someone

- Finding eye contact with a person very intense

- Feeling nervous around, or getting "butterflies" because of someone

- Experiencing sexual arousal: blood rushing to genitals, hard nipples, etc.

- Finding your cheeks flush when you are around someone

---

109. Skip to page 160 to learn about asexual identities more in depth!
110. The experiences on this list are certainly not *always* signs of sexual attraction. These experiences can also be platonic, romantic, sensual, aesthetic or completely random. Not sure what all these words mean? See http://bit.ly/2cmHYaQ or page 139 if you want to learn more now!

- Finding yourself hungry to touch or be close to someone

- Desiring to see a person naked

If you determine you *do* feel sexual attraction, you should know this experience is not uniform or identical for everyone. Different people's sexual attractions are highly diverse. One of the most obvious examples of this is gender preference. For instance, a person could be attracted to only men, only women, both men and women, non-binary people, all genders, and so on. Beyond gender preference though, *intensity* of people's sexual attraction can also vary. One person might describe themselves as being *deeply, fiercely* attracted to men, while another might feel they are only *somewhat* attracted to men. What's more, some people are fluid and find their attractions change over time. There are about a zillion and a half different experiences that exist when it comes to sexual attraction, and what's exciting is, there is a lot of awesome language out there we can use to describe it! This will be most of what the rest of this book will cover.

In the end, everybody gets to decide what is and isn't sexual to them as well as what they find sexually attractive. And that, in a nutshell, is a person's sexual orientation.

Romantic orientation:

Romantic orientation is slightly different...

A person's **romantic orientation** indicates who a person is/isn't romantically attracted to. This can signify:

- What gender(s) they are romantically attracted to

- How intensely/often they experience romantic attraction, if they even experience it at all

- How intensely/often their romantic attractions change/ fluctuate

- The conditions under which they experience romantic attraction

Romantic attraction can be described as an emotional desire, pull towards, and/or attachment to someone.[111] A person who is romantically attracted to someone may desire emotional closeness or intimacy that person. This closeness is commonly described as different or "more than" the intimacy present in friendships or strictly platonic relationships. Like sexual attraction, romantic attraction also varies from person to person because "romance" is -- you guessed it -- subjective. If you're curious about what kinds of acts some people consider romantic, I've conducted a very credible, indisputably scientific Twitter poll, and found the following:

Some things people find romantic include—

· Random hugs

· Forehead kisses

· A sense of humor

· Vulnerability

· Compatibility

· Reliability

· Video game dates with cake

· Establishing trust

· Sex[112]

· Working as a team through stressful situations

· When your partner gently plays with your hair while spooning

---

111. Some people don't think "romantic attraction" is the most accurate way to describe these feelings. They argue that "romance" is a recent Western invention created to spread capitalism and oppress women. They offer "emotional attraction" as an alternative. However, because "romance" is currently so widely implemented, and because many readers likely identity with having a "romantic orientation" and/or "romantic attraction(s)" this book will use the terms "romance/romantic."
112. If seeing "sex" on this list made you scratch your head, let's unpack this a bit: People can find sex romantic in a few ways. For example, it might be a *strictly* romantic experience for someone. They might participate in sex because they enjoy the intimacy and emotional closeness it creates with their partner, not because they are turned on. Alternatively, sex might be *both* a romantic and sexual experience for someone, meaning they enjoy the intimate, emotional connection it creates while simultaneously feeling sexually aroused...Also, sex can be purely sexual, with no romantic connection or feelings at all!

- When your partner notices your phone battery is low and plugs it in for you without being asked

- Farting contests

- Spamming your boo with heart emojis #MuchLove #VeryRomance

As you can see, the scope of what people consider "romantic" is very wide. It's also entirely possible to experience low, no, or a fluctuating amount of romantic attraction. Many people like this identify as being on the aromantic spectrum.[113] In the end, who you're attracted to romantically (if anyone), as well as the intensity and frequency of that attraction, is what helps determine your romantic orientation.

113. Skip to page 161 to learn about aromantic identities more in depth!

How are sexual orientations and romantic orientations different?

Society often conflates sexual and romantic orientations, but the reality is, they can be very different. While these two orientations can certainly interplay and overlap, and for many they do, they can also be entirely separate.[114] For example, a person might be interested in all kinds of genders romantically, but only have sexual interest in one particular gender. My personal sexual and romantic orientations for instance, do not altogether align. You see, I'd label my sexual orientation "pansexual," and my romantic orientation "homoflexible."

For me, being "pansexual," means I find all kinds of genders sexy. Some features I'm sexually drawn to are: short hair, tattoos, vibrant eyes, freckles, strong bodies, curves, kind smiles, a sense of adventure, passion, talent, and confidence. If all these attributes exist in a person, whether they ID as a man, woman, agender, non-binary, or whatever gender, chances are, I'll think they are damn smokin'! I might want to kiss them, touch them, and I probably wouldn't complain if they decided to take off their shirt and show off their abs. These are the kinds of people I am sexually attracted to.

Romantically however, I'm primarily interested in women (this is the "homo" part of "homoflexible"). There's just something about a woman's energy and tenderness that, compared to other genders, more often makes my heart flutter. I also tend to desire serious, love-based relationships with women whom I'm romantically attracted to.

My romantic attractions aren't *exclusive* to women however. There have been exceptions to my primary attraction in the past, as I have romantically fallen for a handful of men (this is the "flexible" part of "homoflexible"). These occurrences are few and far between though, and that is how I know my sexual and romantic orientations are distinct.

My friend Joe is another excellent illustration of a person with non-aligning sexual and romantic orientations. Here is his story.[115]

From a very young age, I knew I wasn't attracted to girls, romantically or sexually. When you're little you already know what it is to be "gay,"

114. Some people call this a "mixed orientation."
115. Find more Joe here: http://bit.ly/2cHscGW

that is, you know you are the "other." So I assumed I was gay for a long time. With adolescence however, I realised that my attraction to men was less than forthcoming. Not only was I unable to imagine any kind of "normative" life with a man in my future, I couldn't picture what an intimate relationship would be like. While I think some of this might have been down to internalized homophobia, it was an extremely difficult time for me between the ages of 14 and 18. I didn't feel gay, let alone straight, bi, etc., and so I couldn't come to terms with any label, even one as pejorative as "homo" at the time. I suffered from a long bout of mental health issues as I was stuck in this limbo state of identity.

Later, exposure to the idea of asexuality allowed me to see myself in a different frame. The crushes I felt towards the same gender didn't have to clash/conflict with a lack of desire to sexually act upon them. In fact, it was perfectly normal to have sexual and romantic attraction function in separate ways. I felt liberated, at ease, and finally able to articulate my identity in a way that is valid for me, rather than measure up to some assumed "homonorm."[116] While I experience a lack of sexual attraction across the board, my homoromanticism leads me to identify both as ace and gay. Although this is accurate, it can be confusing for myself and others due to the very distinct cultures and assumptions about the two identities, yet I must continue to try and make the two sing together.

As you thumb through the pages of this book and start cataloging the plethora of orientations that exist, remember, it is entirely possible for you to feel sexually drawn to someone without feeling romantically drawn to them, and vice versa.[117]

---

116. See the cheat sheet for more on norms!

117. Fun fact: there are also many other kinds of attractions, besides just sexual and romantic! Some of these include:

- **Aesthetic attraction**: Appreciation of someone's appearance that's not inherently linked to sex or romance. *(Example: "THAT PERSON LOOKS SO GOOD. I like their outfit, hair, face, and their body is rockin'!" "Go ask them out!" "Oh no, I don't want to kiss them or date them or anything...just admire them from afar."*

- **Platonic attraction**: Feeling drawn to someone because you crave friendship, familiarity, and/or emotional closeness with them.

- **Sensual attraction**: Appealing to one's senses (most notably touch and smell) in a way that is not inherently linked to sex or romance. If you are sensually attracted to someone you might for example, be attracted to the way they smell. You also might want to hold their hand or cuddle them because you are attracted to the way they feel.

- **Alterous attraction**: Craving an emotional closeness to someone that's not quite platonic nor romantic. *(Example: I don't want to be romantic or sexual with you, but I do want to be emotionally intimate with you in a way that's different from with my friends.)*

If you want to learn even more about these attractions check out: http://bit.ly/2cmHYaQ

Part 3:

SEXUAL AND ROMANTIC IDENTITIES

CHAPTER 4:

Identities and Terms

By this point you've gained a basic understanding of what sexual and romantic orientations are and how they contrast. Great! Next, let's jump into learning about some sexual and romantic identities, as well as some specific orientation labels, prefixes, and suffixes, and what they mean![118]

Single gender attraction:

We'll start with orientations and identities involving attraction to a single gender.

Mono-: **Monosexuality/romanticism means a person is attracted to one gender.**

(Example: My best friend Emily identifies as a woman who is only attracted to men. Alternatively, my fiancée is a woman whose core attraction is to other women. Both of them are only attracted to one gender, and thus, both of them could describe their attractions as being monosexual.)

Important things to note about this prefix:

- Typically it is used as a descriptor rather than an orientation people actively claim for themselves.

- Some people find this term problematic for various reasons:

  - They feel it lumps LGBTQIA+ people who experience single gender attraction in with straight people. This can be upsetting because LGBTQIA+ people do not have the same privileges as straight people. It erases and invalidates the adversity they face.

  - The term has a history of being used in a pejorative or insulting way towards people who experience single gender attraction, implying they are not "queer enough."

  - Some people feel this term is too often used to label others without their consent, which they feel is wrong.[119]

Hetero-/Straight: **Being attracted to the other binary gender.**[120]

118. All of these prefixes/suffixes and labels can be applied to both sexual and romantic orientations.
119. I asked both Grace and Emily if I could describe their attractions as monosexual. Each of them said they were comfy with it!
120. You will note I used the word "other," rather than "opposite." I'm noting this to emphasize that

(Example: As she is a woman only attracted to men, Emily, from the previous example, could be considered straight/hetero.)

Homo-: **Homosexuality/romanticism[121] is when a person is attracted to the same or similar[122] gender(s) as their own.**

(Example: Women who are sexually attracted to women could be considered homosexual.)

Lesbian: This term is commonly used to refer to **women who are attracted to other women.** However, some non-binary and/or genderqueer people who feel a connection to womanhood and who are attracted to women, also identify with this term.

Gay: This label has a few uses.

1. It can be used to refer specifically to **men who are attracted to men.**

2. It can be used to refer to **people who are primarily attracted to the same or similar gender as their own.** *(Example: gay men and lesbians.)*

3. Additionally, some use it as an **umbrella term for anyone not straight.[123]** *(Example: lesbian, bisexual, pansexual, queer, novosexual people, etc.)*

While at first glance many people would consider my lovely fiancée a lesbian, Grace actually prefers the identifier "gay." Here is why.[124]

When I first came out, I was unaware of the many different LGBTQIA+ identifiers that existed. As a nineteen-year-old, who had spent 13 years in Catholic, private school, I was somewhat uneducated regarding the LGBTQIA+ community. So, when I started coming out on a regular basis, I used one of the only labels I knew, "lesbian."

---

language like "opposite" perpetuates the binary. There are no "opposite" genders, even in the binary. Men and women are not opposites, simply two members of the binary.

121. Some feel "homosexuality" is a dated and medicalized term that is falling out of favor in common LGBTQIA+ linguistics.

122. The word "similar" is necessary to keep this definition inclusive of non-binary individuals. This is because nb identities are so diverse; thus finding two nb people with the *exact* same gender is rare. These people still sometimes claim this term if it feels like a good fit however.

123. Some people dislike when "gay" is utilized this way because they feel it erases other identities in the LGBTQIA+ community and/or prioritizes the experiences of gay people over others. *(Example: Saying "gay pride" instead of "pride" or "gay rights" instead of "LGBTQIA+ rights" doesn't acknowledge multisexual, trans, asexual, etc. people)*

124. Find more Grace here: http://bit.ly/2cJN1lW

I still use this term to describe myself from time to time, but it's no longer my go-to qualifier. For me, "lesbian" doesn't totally fit. This is because, the term implies I'm a woman, and some days I don't feel totally feminine. I actually vary a bit on the gender spectrum, so "lesbian" can feel like limitation on my gender.

Nowadays, I prefer the label "gay" because I feel like it doesn't limit my gender to being exclusively female. I think it's important that you use identifiers that make you comfortable, not ones that society would typically associate you with. In my case, a lack of education forced me into a box that didn't fit. Now I embrace self-identification more and use labels that make me feel good. Currently, I am a student of identities and mine might continue to change.

Like my fiancée, I also utilize "gay" to describe myself from time to time. I claim this label even though I'm attracted to genders other than my own. It's hard to explain why it feels right to me. Perhaps it's because "gay" is easier than "bi" or "pan" for others to consume. Often when I tell people I'm "pan" they need me to explain it, and when I tell people I'm "bi" they ask awkward or invasive questions (*"Which gender do you prefer though?" "Have you like …had sex with both?"*)

"Gay" however, is simple, and most people know what it means. Using this easily consumable term can allow me to escape the stigma and questions attached to other labels. It gives me time and space to breathe and just be. After all, constantly explaining and navigating a complex/lesser known identity in our society can be exhausting. Although it would be fantastic if we could, it's not the job of a LGBTQIA+ person to constantly be educating. Sometimes it becomes too much and that's when we need to practice self-care.[125] For me, that means using a label that's simple, clear-cut, and question free.

Other times I use "gay" because it makes me feel included in the LGBTQIA+ community. Biphobia is a sad reality, and as a result some LGBTQIA+ people are hesitant to include multisexual people in LGBTQIA+ spaces and conversations. Like I said before, some days, frankly I am too tired to deal with this. I don't want my queerness to be questioned, so I just say I'm "gay."

The above examples are instances I use "gay" in order to escape stress and scrutiny. There are other times however, when my homoflexible-romanticism makes me feel pretty connected to the label. I'm mainly interested in dating women after all, so "gay" actually feels like a decent and accurate descriptor of me. It all depends on the circumstance and how I'm feeling in a particular moment, but nevertheless, "gay" is indeed an identifier I do claim occasionally.

Multiple gender attractions:

This section covers orientations and identities with attractions to multiple genders. These attractions can range anywhere from two, three, four, to even an infinite number of genders! Get ready, because this section is *much* longer and more diverse than the previous.

Multi-/Non-mono-: **Multisexuality/romanticism and non-monosexuality/romanticism are both descriptors and orientations for attractions to more than one gender.** (*Example: People who are bi, poly, pan, or omnisexual/romantic are all attracted to more than one gender and thus, could be considered multisexual/romantic and/or non-monosexual/romantic.*)

Bi-: Bisexuality/romanticism can mean several things. The two most common definitions include:

---

125. **Self-care**: Making sure one's mind and body stay healthy. This may include acts of love, patience, appreciation performed on oneself, as well as allowing oneself breaks and/or rest, in order to preserve mental clarity and happiness.

1. **Being attracted to two genders.** *(Example: Being attracted to men and women, men and demiguys,*[126] *or maverique and neutrois people.)*

2. **Being attracted to two or more genders.**[127] *(Example: Personally, I am attracted to the same gender as my own, as well as many other genders. This is why "bisexual" is one of the many qualifiers I identify with.)*

Something important to note about this orientation is that bi people do not always experience their attractions to different genders equally or in the same way. Some bi people may have a preference as to which gender they are attracted to most, or they may find they're attracted to different genders in different ways. This is completely valid. Your attraction and/or dating history does not have to be spread out equally across all of the genders that you're attracted to in order to be bi. As with nearly all identity labels, there are no strict rules or requirements for who can claim this identifier. All one needs to do to be bi, is identity this way.

Pan–: **Pansexual/romantic people are capable of being attracted to any or all gender(s).**

Many pan people feel that gender is not a very influential factor in their attraction. This lack of gender-influence on attraction has become commonly associated with pan identity.

Other pan people however, *do* feel gender plays into the way they are attracted to others. Like with bisexuality, some pan people have preferences as to which gender(s) they are most attracted to. Others may be attracted to different genders in different ways.

Bi vs. pan: Often people find themselves confused regarding the difference between bi and pan. In the end, the difference really just comes down to personal preference. For some, there are important distinctions between the two orientations, which is why they use one word over the other. These may include:

---

126. See page 104 for more on the term "demiguys."
127. From my experience, this is how most bisexual people describe their bisexuality. The former definition seems to be falling out of favor in order to more explicitly embrace non-binary people.

Reasons People Use Bi:	Reasons People Use Pan:
Because they want to combat the negative stigma surrounding the label "bi."	To avoid the negative stigma surrounding "bisexual."
Because they wish to help eradicate bi erasure.	Because gender doesn't play a major role in attraction for them. They acknowledge people's gender, but it doesn't make them more or less likely to be attracted to them.
Because they simply feel more connected to the word.	
Because it's the first label they used to describe themselves, and it's the one they are most used to.	
Because they are not attracted to all genders and thus feel "pan" would be inaccurate.	Because the prefix actively challenges a strict gender binary.
Because they feel the public is more familiar with "bi" than "pan." It requires less explaining.	Because it's less known than "bi." This gets people's attention and starts conversations about sexual/romantic diversity.
Because the word "bi" has a long and rich history many people take pride in.	
Because bisexual communities are often more present in physical LGBTQIA+ spaces. Pansexuality however, is still relatively new, and as a result pan communities are found more online.	Because it just feels right.
Because it just feels right.	

Hopefully this chart helps you gain a better understanding as to why different people might prefer either "bi" or "pan." However, I often find that the best way to truly grasp how and why people form connections to certain labels is by listening to their personal stories. One of my closest YouTube friends, Alayna Fender, has some interesting thoughts regarding which words she utilizes for herself. Here are her feelings.[128]

As a woman who finds herself attracted to men, women, and all other genders, there are several identifiers that could "fit" me. I identify as bisexual. However, I feel like the common definition of pansexual describes me more. Within myself though, I am queer.[129] I've had an ever-changing relationship with these labels.

---

128. Find more Alayna here: http://bit.ly/2cJMAIn
129. Curious to learn more about the identifier "queer?" Flip to page 171!

When I first came out, and still to this day, the identifier I use most often is "bi". I find it the simplest, and the easiest for others to consume. However, I believe that the pansexual label is much more fitting for me and my personal sexuality because it actively acknowledges (in it's label) genders other than "male" and "female". Nonetheless, the identifier I have always felt the most connected to is "queer". Even before I was out, I would roll the word around in my mind and feel at home.

So why, then, identify myself as bisexual if I connect more with pansexual and queer? The word bisexual is easily understood, for the most part, by the general public. When I label myself bisexual, there is minimal explaining for me to do. Coming out as pansexual, over and over again, requires me to educate others, over and over again. I don't always feel like carrying that responsibility.

That leaves a final question. Why not identify as queer? Honestly, this is a question I still struggle with. The simple answer is; I don't feel queer enough. I am feminine presenting, and in a long-term relationship with a man. I have straight passing privilege in my relationship and my day-to-day life. I struggle with the possibility that I am appropriating the queer label from those who fought so hard to claim it.

When all's said and done, I identify as bisexual, I feel like the common definition of pansexual describes me better, but within myself, I am queer.

Clearly, Alayna feels distinctions between these words that hold significance for her. Alternatively, other people (including myself) feel the differences between the prefixes are negligible. They might identify with both words and/or use them interchangeably. Whatever the case, there is no right or wrong reason for a person to identify as either "bi" or "pan."

Omni-: Omnisexual/romantic people, like pansexual/romantic people, are also **capable of being attracted to any or all gender(s).** Some omni people use this label (as opposed to other multisexual labels) because they feel gender often *does* play a role in their attractions, and this label is commonly associated with gender-influenced attraction. While not all omni people feel this way, some describe themselves as being drawn to different genders in different ways, to different degrees, and/or for different reasons.

Christi is an omnisexual individual and below she describes how her attractions to different genders occur differently.[130]

I feel that the term omnisexual suits me because I am capable of attraction to people of any gender (or someone with a lack of gender), but I am attracted to different genders in different ways. I think a lot of this has to do with the fact that I'm also demisexual, so I don't experience attraction to anyone unless I first have a strong emotional bond with them. With most people I've been attracted to, the attraction develops after we become pretty close friends. However, whenever I've been attracted to women, that attraction has developed much later, after we'd become extremely close friends. So, essentially, the variation in attraction I experience towards people of different genders is dependent upon timing.

Poly-: **Attraction to multiple, but not necessarily all, genders.** *(Example: Marco is attracted to men, non-binary people, and agender people. He is not attracted to women, and he is unsure whether or not he is attracted to other genders. He might consider himself polysexual.)*

Bicurious: If a person is bicurious, they are **curious about having sexual/romantic attractions and/or experiences with more than one gender.**

---

130. Find more Christi here: http://bit.ly/2ce2vcI

Tri-: A trisexual/romantic person is someone who has an **attraction to three genders** (*Example: Being attracted to men, women, and neutrois people.*)

Try-: People who are trysexual/romantic are often described as willing to "try anything once." Essentially, they are **open to experimenting.**

Important things to note about this identity:

- This is more of an identity word which describes a sexual/romantic openness rather than an orientation.

- This word is often used in different contexts and different ways. Often it is thrown around in joking and/or derogatory ways, however, we need to remember that for some it's a serious, legitimate way of describing identity.

-flexible: This is a suffix that indicates a person has a **typical, primary type of attraction; however, they acknowledge and leave room for possible exceptions.** Adding a prefix to this word can offer more information as to what the person's typical attraction is. (*Example: Romantically, I identify as homoflexible. This means that usually I'm attracted to women. However, I have fallen in love with men in the past.*)

Lindsey Doe is a teacher of sexology and also the host of "Sexplanations," an excellent sex positive Youtube channel, who describes her orientation as flexible.[131]

Since middle school I've wished that I was a lesbian. I'd even pretend to have lesbian relationships with my friends where we'd talk about what I thought were lesbian topics in what I perceived as lesbian voices. Looking back, it was silly, but really telling. At the time my urges were toward boys, I dated guys, and felt funny in my loins around Brian not Jenny, but identifying as heterosexual didn't fit so I forced alternatives, and role played as a 12-year-old lesbian.

Heterosexuality as a label still doesn't fit. I loathe the rigidity of it and the limits it puts on my sexuality, but identifying as bi-, pan-, homo- etc. wouldn't feel honest. I am cis-female who experiences sexual and romantic attraction to men. That's how it's been since puberty.

---

131. Find more Lindsey here: http://bit.ly/1hDKcg7

So when I learned about and adopted the label heteroflexible, I became more comfortable. I could accept the history of my orientation while holding space for it to adjust to new experiences and go anywhere I let it. To me, flexibility means that I truly understand the dynamics of sexuality including my own. I acknowledge my attractions but stay open to their movement. It's not black or white. It's not said and done. It's flexible.

Noma–: This is a **sexual/romantic attraction to anyone who isn't a man.**

Nowoma–: This is a **sexual/romantic attraction to anyone who isn't a woman.**

Skolio/Cetero–:[132] Skoliosexual/romantic and ceterosexual/romantic people are **attracted to people of non-binary (nb) genders.**

Important things to note about this orientation:

- Some interpret this orientation as an exclusive attraction to nb people, while others interpret it as being capable of attraction to nb people.

- There is heavy debate regarding whether or not these labels are problematic.

  - Some people feel the labels fetishize[133] nb individuals.

  - Other people believe only nb people should be allowed to identify this way.

  - Some people dislike the prefix "skolio," as it means crooked or bent. They feel this implies skolio people and/or non-binary people are unnatural, wrong, or "twisted" in some way. Thus the prefix "cetero," meaning "other," came about.

  - Skolio/cetero is often mistaken or misinterpreted as an attraction to androgyny, which it's not. This becomes an issue when it perpetuates a stereotype of nb people. After

---

132. The reason I've placed this orientation in this section of the book, as opposed to the "attraction to a single gender" section, is because non-binary identities include a vast multitude of genders, and therefore skolio/cetero people are often attracted to more than one gender.

133. Fetishize: to have an extreme sexual, obsessive, or committed preference or attachment towards something. Often fetishizing people is seen as problematic because it reduces people to one quality and dehumanizes them.

all, you can't tell if someone is nb by appearance because gender identity is very different from gender expression.

You know what – This is such a complicated identity let's hear what another nb person, besides myself has to say about it. I give you Sage, a hella smart, bigender youtuber.[134]

I have mixed feelings about this orientation. On the one hand, I don't want to police the way people identify their sexualities. If a person feels that they are attracted to non-binary folks, either exclusively or in addition to other forms of attraction, then that's perfectly legitimate. I'm a non-binary person who identifies as pansexual, and because I'm attracted to people of all different genders I've never felt the need to specify my attraction to non-binary folks. In that way, I acknowledge that I do not really understand the experience of someone who identifies as skolio/cetero.

However, I do worry that this identity may lead to the fetishization or generalization of non-binary people. As Ashley stated before, you cannot tell that someone is non-binary just by looking at them. So, what does it mean to be attracted to non-binary folks? We're a very diverse group of people who express their genders in many different ways. Is this orientation about attraction to the stereotypical non-binary person mentioned above? If not, then what is it based on?

I have to admit that I would feel uncomfortable if someone expressed that they were attracted to me because I'm non-binary. I think I would feel a

134. Find more Sage here: http://bit.ly/2bXJ649

bit fetishized, like the person was into me because of my gender identity rather than because of who I am. If I could have a conversation with them, however, and find out what they meant, that could potentially help to ease my discomfort.

There are people who are exclusively attracted to women. There are people who are exclusively attracted to men. If we have folks who express their attraction to binary genders, then maybe having folks express attraction to non-binary genders is okay. I think that there are likely ways of expressing this attraction which are objectifying and ways which are not.

After reading Sage's story, one of the editors of this book brought up an interesting point in regards to Sage not wanting to police people's identities. She said, "Policing isn't fundamentally harmful to the community. Sometimes, we need to bash back against fetishism."

Another editor chimed in and also brought up an interesting point, "The one question that kept surfacing [as I read] is that we can't tell how ANYONE identifies [just] by looking at them, so what do we mean when we say we are attracted to women? To men? Don't the same troubling pieces of this identity (skolio/ceterosexuality) surface with the others (heterosexuality, homosexuality, etc.)? It's incredibly complicated!"

Incredibly complicated indeed! And this skolio/cetero analysis has become *incredibly* long! Goes to show how complex and powerful identity words can be. In the end, all we can do is our best when deciding which words we support and utilize. We can research, learn, listen, and keep an open mind. After that, we just have to go with our gut, and do what feels right.

Before we completely move on, let's hear from someone who claims this label. Douglas is an English teacher and gay man who identifies with this term. Here is why he uses "skolio" for himself.[135]

In college, I made a friend on whom I had feelings I struggled to identify. As a gay man, I was supposed to be interested only in men, but she did not identify as a man. These feelings made me ashamed of myself, because I assumed I was interested in her masculine energy and ignoring her actual identity. This was not an isolated incident—I frequently found myself

---

135. Find more Douglas here: http://bit.ly/2coROYA

drawn to people with trans and non-binary gender identities, often before I even knew what those identities were.

Then at the end of 2014, Ashley posted the first ABCs of LGBT video. In it, she defined the term "skoliosexual." At the time, I ignored it—I was definitely gay. No question there. But then I met another wonderful new non-binary friend, and those old feelings resurfaced—feelings I could now identify specifically as romantic attraction. I didn't want to have sex with them as I wasn't sexually attracted to them, but I definitely wanted to make out with them and do other romantic things! Unfortunately, most of the definitions of "skoliosexual" I could find had an exclusionary definition: attracted to non-binary individuals and only non-binary individuals—and I knew I was sexually attracted to men. But I couldn't deny the very real feelings I had for some of the trans people in my life. Luckily, I don't have to have only one label—I can identify as homosexual and skolioromantic at the same time.

For people who experience attraction towards nb people, but are concerned about identifying as skolio/cetero because of its potential problems, perhaps consider the following term:

Diamoric: This is a descriptor that has two primary uses; to describe someones's identity, and to describe a relationship.

In terms of personal identity, a non-binary person may identify as "diamoric" **to emphasize their own non-binary identity and their attraction to/relationship(s) with other non-binary people.** It's important to note that this term was made *only* for non-binary people to use this way.

One of the biggest differences between "diamoric" and "skolio/cetero," is that skolio/cetero are sexual orientations. Diamoric is not an orientation. It's an identity word that can be used in conjunction with one's orientation. *(Example: A genderfluid person who is bisexual may identify as a diamoric bisexual to emphasize their own non-binary identity and their attraction to/relationship with other non-binary people. A demigirl lesbian may identify as a diamoric lesbian to emphasize their own non-binary identity and their attraction to/relationship with non-binary people.)*

In terms a relationship, **a diamoric relationship is one that involves at least one non-binary person.** Usage of the word "diamoric" in this sense isn't only restricted to non-binary people. A relationship can be diamoric even if one of the members is binary. *(Example: If in the future Douglas from the previous story were in a relationship with a non-binary person, he could refer to that relationship as a diamoric relationship if he wanted to.)*

For those interested in how diamoric came about, the term was invented because current descriptors like "gay" or "straight" didn't seem to accurately describe relationships between or involving non-binary people. Since non-binary identities are so diverse, it's rare to find two non-binary people with the *exact* same gender. This is why "gay" (to describe nb people especially interested in and/or attracted to other nb people) isn't always a good fit.

And although many non-binary people have different genders, they are not necessarily "opposite." Some can be very similar. This is why "straight" isn't always a good fit either.

"Diamoric" comes from the greek prefix "dia," meaning "passing through," "going apart," and "thoroughly/completely" and the latin "amor" for love. Thus, the word "diamoric" encompasses all love/attractions/relationships that pass through, go apart from, or completely encompass the gender spectrum.

This brings us to the end of this section. Next, let's learn about some of the fluid attractions people can experience.

Fluid attractions:

For many people, sexual and romantic attractions are constantly changing. Shifts in a person's orientation may occur gradually over a lifetime or drastically within just a few days. These changes can occur rarely, constantly, or somewhere in between. The potential for fluidity in our orientations is amazing, and luckily there are some labels that embrace this!

Fluid: If a person's attractions or orientations are fluid, this simply means they **experience change.** How fluid someone is depends on the person and their circumstance.

Being fluid could feel like the following:

- An ocean.[136] Your attractions might come in strong, powerful, shifting waves. You might feel the peaks and valleys of these waves deeply and constantly.

- A river. Your attractions might run straight, smooth and predictably for a hundred miles until they hit an obstacle and suddenly change their course.[137]

- A stream draining into a lake. A person's attractions might be strong and flowing for a time until they suddenly gather, come to a slow, or completely stop.

- A waterfall. Fluid attractions aren't required to always change in smooth, shifting ways. You can also rise or fall immediately from one level, or kind of attraction, to another, like a waterfall.

Abro-: An abrosexual/romantic person **experiences a fluid and/or changing orientation.** This means the object(s) (e.g. men, women, nb people, multiple genders, nobody) of their attractions can change as well as the intensity of their attractions.

Abrosexuality/romanticism could be considered a form of fluidity. However, many people who use this word, do so because, "fluidity" can be applied to *both* one's general sexual orientation and specific

---

136. PUN!

137. You know, "like a stream that meets a boulder halfway through the wood!" ...I couldn't help myself.

objects of attractions. "Abro" however, is *more specific to orientation*. In other words, it's not just one's attractions or preferences that shift. *(Example: "I like men and woman but my preference changes depending on the day.")*, but rather their *entire orientation* that changes. *(Example: An abrosexual person might switch between feeling straight one day, and pansexual or asexual on other days.)*

Here is Lauren to tell us about her experience identifying with this orientation.[138]

From about age 10, I knew that something was "up" with my sexuality. It seemed to change so frequently that I was honestly scared that I'd never work out what was going on.

My questioning period led me to the depths of Tumblr– just by chance I stumbled across one of the very few "master posts" that included "abrosexuality." I really related to the idea of constantly changing sexuality. I quickly realised that my "gay days" and "straight days" and "pan days" and "ace days" and all the other feelings I experienced weren't me being weird (even though I'd spent 7 years telling myself that). Actually I had a totally valid identity. One that other people experienced too!

Today, I am happy with my identity, and have embraced every part of my sexuality. I have experienced a few negative responses, mainly from within the LGBTQIA+ community. For example, once a cis gay man told me, "Abro is just a hipster word for pansexual."[139] I didn't let it bother me though. I've found my label, and I'm very happy to use it.

–flux: In regards to orientation, "flux," is a suffix that indicates **that a person's attractions fluctuate in amount or intensity.** Usually a prefix is placed in front of "flux," which can indicate more information about the genders that a person's attractions fluctuate between. *(Example: A triflux person may consistently stay attracted to the same three genders but their preferences may fluctuate.)*

---

138. Find more Lauren here: http://bit.ly/2bWpPel
139. A few years ago, I was explaining my orientation to someone and they told me, "pansexuality is just bisexuality in pretentious wrapping paper." This memory resurfaced upon reading Lauren's experience being told her orientation was just "a hipster word for pansexual." It's interesting to see how public/outside opinions of identity words shift over time. "Pansexuality" was being referenced as more standard/commonplace in Lauren's story, but only a few years earlier it was very new, misunderstood, and not widely utilized. Personally, I think the take away from this is that, public/outside opinion of identifiers and orientations will always be changing. The person who matters most though, when deciding if a label is a good fit, is the person in question.

-spike: Spike is similar to flux. It is also a suffix that indicates a person's attractions fluctuate. However, spike-identifying people **often feel they experience no attraction (ie. that they are aromantic/aro or asexual/ace), but then suddenly and intensely experience a spike in attraction(s)** for a period of time. *(Examples of usages: arospike and acespike, which would denote the person experiences no romantic attraction and then some/lots of attraction, or no sexual attraction and then some/lots of attraction, respectively.)*

Novo-: This orientation was originally created for genderfluid and multigender people. A novosexual/romantic person's **attractions change based on the gender(s) they are experiencing.** *(Example: a genderfluid, novosexual person may identify as a lesbian when they are a woman, but identity as pansexual when they are non-binary. This is partly due to the way many sexual orientations include gender identity assumptions within them-- like for example how lesbians are automatically assumed to be women.)*

We've reached the end of this section, well done! You have just learned a *lot* about multiple gender attractions. Before we move on, I'd like to quickly touch on why learning about these identities is so necessary. Orientations with attractions to multiple genders are important to understand because they are frequently misrepresented, erased, and questioned. This often leads to stigma, phobias, and skepticism surrounding these identities.

Bi erasure is one prominent example of this. Bi erasure is when insufficient representation of bi people is provided, or when the existence of bi people is totally invalidated. *Real* examples of *real* bi erasure that *real* bi people face, include:

- *"You're really bi? Really? Well, when was the last time you hooked up with a guy?"*

- *"I would sleep with a bi guy, but I'd never date one – I mean they're not really bi, they're just horny cheaters."*

- *"Why don't you just choose men, it's easier and you've done it before. You will only end up with one anyways."*

- *"I feel like being bi is a stepping stone that all lesbians go through – just wait, you'll see."*

- *"Every girl has small crushes on other girls. That's normal. You're not bi."*

- *"Haven't you had girlfriends in the past though? And lots of girl crushes?" "Yea I did! And lots of guy crushes too! I was just in denial of them." "No, no, no that doesn't sound like you!"*

- *"Which side are you backing these days?"*

- *"If you're not ROMANTICALLY attracted to women you can't call yourself bi."*

- *"This is my friend Ben. He's gay." "Actually, I'm bisexual." "You know what I mean."*

- *"As far as I'm concerned, you're straight, with the possibility of kinky threesomes."*

Constantly combating comments like these and convincing the world your sexuality is legitimate can be exhausting. It's not only bi people who face erasure like this though, all multisexual/romantic identities do. On top of erasure, multisexual/romantic orientations also face a hefty amount of stigma surrounding them. Our culture tends to associate being attracted to more one gender with a multitude of negative characteristics, such as being greedy, confused, unfaithful, sex-crazed, attention-seeking, and trendy. This stigma causes many multisexual/romantic people to remain closeted or feel ashamed of their orientation which is truly unfortunate. Everyone deserves to be comfortable and proud of who they are!

What is important to remember is that all of these identities are valid and should not be stereotyped. The more we learn about and accept these orientations, the less we will encounter harmful sentiments like the aforementioned ideas and comments.

Asexual and aromantic identities:

You've now arrived at the asexuality and aromanticism portion of the book! This section will cover people who experience little to no sexual and/or romantic attraction. Earlier I said that "spectrums" would be my favorite subject covered in the text, but I'm torn. Ace and aro topics are also very special to me as I have many close, personal friends belonging to this community. I find the vast amount of diversity and the profound understanding they possess fascinating and beautiful.

Asexual: An umbrella term and/or stand-alone identifier for **people who do not experience sexual attraction to varying degrees.**

Ace: This term can be used as both:

- An umbrella term for **any identity that falls on the asexual spectrum.**

- **A shorthand for asexual.**

Amelia is one of my favorite LGBTQIA+ YouTubers and this is what being asexual is like for her.[140]

Realizing you're asexual is a little bit like discovering everything you were told about adulthood was a lie. Or, in my case, that my adult life was not going to pan out like an episode of "Friends". Until I started to explore my

---

140. Find more Amelia here: http://bit.ly/1R3f35K

asexuality, I always figured that everyone ended up with the sex life of a sitcom character. Hooks ups, followed by some great romance in which I would fall into the arms of a faceless man or woman and sex would not only be expected, but desired. Asexuality complicated that vision.

When you're asexual, the desires and urges you're promised in sex education never come. You don't feel sexual attraction, so you're shut out of so much of our sex-driven culture right from the get go. As an asexual person your relationship with sex is complicated, and you probably won't have the same kind of sex life as your peers. This can be difficult to come to terms with — it was for me.

With that being said, however, being asexual has been overwhelmingly positive experience. The community is full of creative people and I've learned a lot about human sexuality more broadly through learning about asexuality. Having a word to describe my sexual orientation has left me more confident, more comfortable in myself, and more willing to explore other parts of my identity like my gender expression and romantic orientation. Strange as it may sound to some, I like being asexual. I wouldn't change a thing.

Aromantic: An umbrella term and/or stand-alone identifier, for **people who do not experience romantic attraction to varying degrees.**

Aro: This term can be used as both:

- An umbrella term for **any identity that falls on the aromantic spectrum.**

- **A shorthand for aromantic.**

Before we continue, remember that sexual and romantic orientations can be separate. I want to reiterate this to ensure it's understood that someone can be ace without being aro, and vice versa. While these orientations might be linked for some, they can also be totally independent for others.

I'd also like to make it clear that "being without sex and/or romance," is not the same as "being without love." In order to illustrate this, here is Jonah to tell you about his aromanticism.[141]

In my experience of bringing the word "aromantic" into conversation, most people initially picture a heartless person, who is incapable of expressing love or being in any form of a relationship. With all of the negative stereotypes and misinformation about aromantic people, it can be incredibly difficult to get a proper idea of what aromanticism actually consists of. For me, being aromantic means that I don't experience romantic attraction.

141. Find more Jonah here: http://bit.ly/2ce1gdv

That does not limit me from experiencing other forms of attraction however, such as aesthetic attraction and platonic attraction.[142] *And while I can't experience romantic love, I still have a big heart full of other forms of love, such as familial and platonic.*

For years, I believed I couldn't be aromantic because I knew I wanted companionship, and I thought the only way to have that was through a romantic relationship. My understanding of romantic attraction blurred with platonic and aesthetic attractions, and it was difficult for me to keep everything straight.

It wasn't until I found a blog post titled "You May Be Aromantic If..." that everything finally started to click in my mind. Finally, all of the negative stereotypes and misinformation I previously knew about aromanticism disappeared, and I was able to understand it on an entirely new level. After I had access to accurate information about aromanticism, I was able to recognize and accept myself as an aromantic person, and I have to say, it was incredibly liberating.

At this point, you've gained better insight as to what it means to be asexual and aromantic, and you might find yourself wondering, is there a label for people who *do* experience sexual and romantic attractions? There is!

Zed-/Allo-: **Someone who experiences sexual and/or romantic attractions**, a.k.a. anyone *not* ace/aro.

Important things to note about these labels:

- "Allo" is probably the most popular and common term to refer to people who aren't ace/aro, but some feel it is problematic for the following reasons:

  - Semantically, the term is more opposite to "autosexual"[143] than it is to "ace" or "aro."

  - Some argue this term is rooted in clinical sexology. Because clinical sexology has had a history of oppressing ace/aro individuals, many take issue with using a word with such strong clinical sexological associations.

---

142. See page 139 for more on aesthetic and platonic attraction!
143. See page 173 for more on autosexuality!

- "Zed" was created as an alternative to "allo," and to emphasize that ace/aro identities exist on a spectrum, from a to zed.

- Typically, these words are used as descriptors rather than labels that people actively identify with. Even though these are not usually labels people claim for themselves, these words are still very useful. Having terms for people who aren't ace/aro helps facilitate discussion of people who aren't ace/aro without presenting them as "the norm." In other words, it helps us avoid the trap of thinking, "There are ace/aro people and there are normal people."

As mentioned earlier in this book; asexuality and aromanticism exist on a spectrum. Now that you've learned about the ends of the spectrum (ace/aro and zed/allo) let's explore some the identities that exist in the nebulous space in between.

Gray-:[144] Graysexual/romantic people can include, but are not limited to:

- **People who experience very low amounts of attraction**

- **People who experience attraction rarely or only under certain conditions**

- **People who are not sure whether they experience attraction.**

Below Eli shares their experience identifying as graysexual.[145]

My name is Eli and I identify as gray asexual. For me, this term means that I very rarely experience sexual attraction. I remember being little and first learning about sexual attraction. Like most young kids learning about sex, I was shocked and kind of confused. I do remember thinking that I'd never want to do experience that; it honestly just sounded so unappealing to me. I figured that those thoughts would change as I got older though because that's what people always told me.

I think the first time I questioned whether I was on the asexual spectrum was during a conversation I had with my mom. I'd just finished my annual physical with my doctor and as per usual, she asked whether I

---

144. There are many alternative spellings and slang versions of this term. Some of these include: gray asexual/gray-a/grace/gray ace and gray aromantic/grayro.
145. Find more Eli here: http://bit.ly/2chC7lh

was sexually active. Since it was on my mind, I told my mom about how I'd probably never answer "yes" to that question because I simply wasn't interested in having sex. My mom responded with, "You're still young, that will change," and I immediately said, "But what if it doesn't? Maybe I'm asexual!" My mom laughed and dismissed my thought quickly, but I continued to think about it.

I've only experienced sexual attraction a couple of times, which is why I choose to identify with the label gray asexual. When I have experienced sexual attraction, it's with someone who I have formed a strong emotional connection with. I don't experience that kind of attraction towards a stranger or someone I've just met. Sometimes, I find my own identity hard to wrap my mind around and explain because there are a lot of gray and unclear areas. That also may be my favorite part about being gray asexual: the uncertainty. I think it's cool that depending on the person, or my mood, I can feel different things towards someone I really care about. It's kind of like a constant adventure.

Demi-: The most common definition of demisexuality/romanticisim is an orientation in which **a person who only experiences attraction to people with whom they have formed a strong emotional bond.**[146]

I invited Jeff Miller, a popular YouTuber, trans person, and a very talented musician, to share his experience identifying with this label.[147]

Being demisexual and demiromantic to me means that I do not experience sexual or romantic attraction to others until a deep emotional bond has been formed.

For the longest time, I felt like I was broken because I didn't experience attraction the way my friends or my peers did. Even when I was younger, I didn't get how all of my friends were having crushes. I felt left out. I wanted to know what they were talking about and what they were feeling. For some people, it is possible to develop crushes on strangers or

146. However, some people consider demisexual/romantic to mean that they only experience limited sexual/romantic attraction.
147. Find more Jeff here: http://bit.ly/2c3glEf

people they don't know very well, but they often choose not to act on those attractions until they know the person better.

I genuinely do not feel these attractions until a deep emotional bond formed. It's not a choice. It's just the way my feelings happen as they do not exist until that connection occurs for me. I can count on one hand the number of people I've ever been sexually attracted to and I can count on two hands the number of people I've been romantically attracted to in my entire life. This isn't really a common experience. All I know is the day I found out about these identities, something clicked for me. I felt I wasn't broken anymore because I found words that described me and I didn't feel so alone.

Quoisexual/romantic, a.k.a. WTFromantic: This identity has a few common definitions:

- **A person who can't tell the difference between attractions they experience** *(Example: "I think I might be romantically attracted to you? ...But it also might be just platonic...ah, I can't tell if I want to be your good friend or your girlfriend.")*

- **A person unsure if they experience attraction** *(Example: "Is this what it feels like to be sexually attracted to someone? Maybe? ...Also, maybe not.")*

- **A person who doesn't think romantic or sexual attractions are relevant to them** *(Example: "It's not that I'm confused about what attractions I'm feeling, rather I actively disidentify with sexual attraction/ orientation as sensemaking for me.")*

My friend Kai explains their experience with these identities below.[148]

I identify as quoiromantic (or wtfromantic) because my romantic orientation has been a mystery to me for ages. As a kid, I loved the super sweet romance of Disney movies, but when everyone else started having crushes I just felt confused and left out. My first "crush" was on the popular boy everyone else had already had a crush on two years earlier. I was determined to act on this feeling, so I asked to play with him at recess. He decided we should play spies, which I thought was so cool, until his mission for me was to figure out if this girl liked him back. Strangely enough, I wasn't jealous or disappointed. I just thought that was really boring, and the next day I found other kids to play with.

148. Find more Kai here: http://bit.ly/2cxDxWr

I have had maybe 5 crushes in my entire life, and the majority of those ended the same way; I didn't do anything about them, and eventually I realized I just wanted to be closer friends with them. This makes me wonder if they were really crushes at all, or just me projecting my desire for a romantic relationship.

I heard about asexuality as a senior in high school, and that's also when I started questioning my romantic orientation. I knew I was asexual right away, but aromantic didn't quite click. For a while I just pushed it aside because it was too confusing. I was still interested in having a romantic relationship, but didn't know if I experienced romantic attraction or what that even meant. After some research into various arospec (aromantic spectrum) identities, I found the term "wtfromantic" and a whole bunch of people who identified with that. While it can be confusing at times, being able to connect with other people who have similar experiences is really helpful.

Some ace and aro identities not only exist on more than one place on the spectrum, but also experience fluctuations or changes. One of the identities includes...

Ace/aroflux: There are two definitions most commonly associated with this orientation:

- **Having a fluctuating orientation that always stays within the ace spectrum** *(Example: This type of person might feel demisexual one day and totally asexual another day.)*

- **Having an orientation that fluctuates between experiencing lots of attraction, some attraction, and no attraction.**

This brings us to the end of the asexual and aromatic section. Before we move on though I'd like to shed some light on the fact that this is a part of the LGBTQIA+ community that is often very underrepresented and misunderstood, not only by the general public, but within the LGBTQIA+ community as well. To demonstrate this, I encourage you to try and recall the last time you:

- Saw a graysexual character in a TV show

- Read a book with an aromantic character

- Discussed methods for improving ace inclusion in your GSA

- Mentioned asexuality or aromanticism when you were teaching your straight friend about the rainbow of identities under the LGBTQIA+ umbrella

For many of us, the likely answers to these questions are:

- "I actually can't even think of *one* gray character on TV."

- "Aromantic characters? Those exist?"

- "Well, my asexual friend did bring it up once."

- "...Oops."

Because of this regrettable lack of representation, ace and aro people are continuously bombarded by adversity. This can include:

- People questioning the legitimacy of their orientation. *(Example: "Eh, I think being asexual is a choice... or maybe those people simply haven't found the right partner for them yet.")*

- LGBTQIA+ individuals excluding ace and aro people from LGBTQIA+ conversations and spaces. (*Example: "This group is for queer people ...you're basically a straight person who just can't commit to a relationship."*)

- Feeling broken or insufficient in a society that is overwhelming sexually and romantically charged. (*Example: "Come on, just admit it, you have to find SOME people sexy! That's just human nature! It's like in our DNA!"*)

- Corrective therapies. (*Example: "My cousin used to be asexual too, until he started hormone treatments. You could try that? Or maybe therapy?"*)

- Invasive questions. (*Example: "So you've never had sex then...do you, uh, masturbate?"*)

- Slut-shaming and/or accusations of being frigid/prudish/ etc. and inconsiderate of others. (*Example: "Aromantic, as in, no romance but still wanting sex? You're a heartless, sex-crazed monster, who just wants to 'get some' without commitment!"*)

- Serious lack of representation in media. (*Example: "Why would asexual/aromantic people even need representation? They're represented by basically anyone who's not having sex/in a relationship."*)

It's easy to see the daily frustration many ace and aro people face. It seems one of the most critical goals many people in this community have, is simply for more people to be aware and accepting of their identity. In other words, they'd like to be acknowledged and understood.[149] I can't speak for everyone, but to me, that doesn't seem like too much to ask for.

In the end, ace and aro people exist and their identities are legitimate. It's time the LGBTQIA+ community starts including them, and it's time *all* people start becoming more informed about these orientations. This is why I plan for this book's sequel to be heavily ace and aro focused. Currently this section only covers some of the more common identities within these communities

---

149. For those who want to know more, Kristin Russo's video http://bit.ly/1O48oYa touches on this and provides some great intro information about asexuality.

More sexual and romantic identities:

We've almost reached the end of our journey exploring sexual and romantic diversity. The following identities are the last eight identities we will cover. I've included these terms/orientations here because they surpass or go beyond the scope of the other sections in this book. In some cases, this is because the object of these identities' attractions is not gender. Rather, some are focused on elements like presentation or personality.

Queer: Queer is a term used to describe **any identity that is not cisgender and/or not hetero.**

It is a particularly powerful and loaded label. Because of this, I wanted to investigate why different people like or dislike utilizing it. I organized my findings into a chart on the following page.

Do Utilize Queer:	Don't Utilize Queer:
Reclaiming "queer" has proven to be an empowering experience for many LGBTQIA+ people. They feel taking ownership of the word, strips it of its previous malicious power. Others like the ambiguity and/or fluidity built into the label. Some simply like how short and easy to use the word is. Some praise "queer" for being one of the most inclusive umbrella terms. They feel it unifies LGBTQIA+ people under one title while still allowing them to maintain their autonomy with their specific label. "Queer" can be more politically charged than many other LGBTQIA+ labels. Some people like what this word can imply about their political and social goals.	The word has a long history of being a derogatory, hurtful slur for LGBTQIA+ people. Although, many members of the community have recently chosen to reclaim it, the word still packs a hateful punch for some. For these reasons, identifying with it is uncomfortable for them. Other people may not personally have a problem with the word "queer," but they recognize the triggering power it has. They feel removing "queer" from their vocabulary is an easy sacrifice if it means sparing individuals from the painful memories and feelings they experience upon hearing it. Some feel "queer" is a very exclusive term. This is because anytime it's used as an umbrella term for the LGBTQIA+ community, it alienates those who don't identify with it. Some don't like the political and radical connotations sometimes associated with "queer."

Personally, I have a fierce attachment to the word queer, and I welcome any excuse to claim it. This is largely due to the fact I was afraid of the label for a long time. The word's long, hurtful history was at first difficult to ignore, and for a while I questioned if I'd earned the right to use it. I wondered if I was involved in the community enough, if I'd had been out long enough, if I was "gay enough." When I finally did start embracing the label, like many, I felt powerful and liberated. I used it zealously and almost exclusively.

I even used to use the word to describe other people, without asking permission. When I discovered not everyone thought this was appropriate, I was initially resistant to change. Truthfully, even when I started this book, I still found myself using "queer" and "LGBTQIA+" interchangeably. I knew it was uncomfy and triggering for some people, but my selfish affinity for the label, made it hard to give it up. After few months of deliberating, I determined that using "queer" to describe others, including the community as whole, was something I wanted to sacrifice in order to keep everyone feeling safe and included.

However, I will call *myself* queer though, ALL DAY LONG! It's my favorite qualifier, it embodies everything I feel about my sexuality and gender, and when I use the word, I feel a euphoric pride!

Recip-: **Experiencing attraction to someone only after knowing that they are attracted to you.** *(Example: If you are recipromantic, you might form crushes on people whom you discover have a crush on you.)*

Auto-: While autosexuality/romanticism literally translates to "attraction to oneself," I've encountered a several interpretations of this term. Some include:

· **Being able to elicit a sexual/romantic attraction from yourself by yourself.** This is often mistaken for being egotistical or narcissistic, however often autosexual/romantic people's attraction for themselves stems from deep personal introspection and love. Some autosexual/romantic people even carry out relationships with themselves.

· **Not desiring to partake in sexual activity with others but still enjoying being sexually intimate with themselves,** i.e masturbating. This behavior/desire could also fall under several other identities/orientations; it is not exclusive to autosexuality/romanticism. As with any label, even if this describes you, you should only identify with this term if it feels right.

Androgyne-: Someone who is androgynesexual/romantic is **attracted to androgyny.**[150]

Questioning: People who are questioning are **unsure of their sexual/romantic orientation or gender identity.** They may be in the process of exploring and discovering their identity, or they may be content not knowing. A person can remain questioning anywhere from a short period of time to their entire lives.[151]

---

150. For those of you scratching your head thinking, "Haven't I seen this before?" we explored the words "androgyne" and "androgynous" in relation to *gender* and *expression* earlier on pages 118-122. "Androgynesexuality/romanticism" however, is an orientation not a gender/expression.

151. Look, I published a book on sexual/gender diversity....and I still question the specifics of my identity almost every single day.

Woma/gyne-: Womasexuality/romanticism and gynesexuality/romanticism are **attractions to women and/or femininity.**

- This term was originally created for non-binary people. Many prefer these labels, because unlike "lesbian" or "straight," they don't imply misinformation about their own gender. *(Example: A bigender person primarily attracted to women might consider themselves woma/gynesexual.)*

- Important things to note about these orientations:

  - Gynesexual is often used to describe exclusive attraction to vaginas. Although this may not be the intention of the person identifying with the word, many feel prefix "gyne" still has strong associations with genitalia. Thus, people have critiqued this term as exclusionary of trans women.

  - "Woma" came about in an attempt to make a more inclusive alternative.

Ma/Andro-: Masexuality/romanticism and androsexuality/romanticism are **attractions to men and/or masculinity.**

- These terms were also created for non-binary people who felt existing monosexual labels, like "gay" and "straight," implied inaccurate information about their own gender.

- Important things to note about these orientations:

  - Androsexual is often used to describe exclusive attraction to penises. Although this may not be the intention of the person identifying with the word, many feel the prefix "andro" still has strong associations with genitalia. Thus, people have critiqued this term as exclusionary of trans men.

  - "Ma" came about in an attempt to make a more inclusive alternative.

Now if you've never met anyone who identifies like this, today is your lucky day! Here is Josh to tell you about why "androsexual" is his label of choice![152]

---

152. Find more Josh here: http://bit.ly/2bWt8C4

I'm Josh. I'm 20 years old and a writer. I'm also androsexual. That doesn't mean I have a thing for C3PO or NDR-113 from The Positronic Man (though Robin Williams' joyful spirit is enough to make anyone weak at the knees and warm inside); it means that I am attracted to men. If I still identified as male, I'd probably be a flaming homosexual, but that's far from the most accurate label I could find. If you're agender, gender-fluid or anything outside the gender binary, "homosexual" doesn't quite fit. It can even be quite restrictive – like an ill-fitting jumper, or a uniform several sizes too small.

Besides, I said I was attracted to men, and while that's not a lie, it's not completely true, either. It's masculinity that I find so alluring, and that's something that can belong to anyone whether they be male, female, non-binary, or trans, regardless of genitalia. By choosing "androsexual" over "homosexual" or "gay," I feel as though I acknowledge and recognize the complexities of gender and sexuality and how it is more nuanced than I once believed – a fact I now endeavor not to forget.

I was unsure whether to classify andro/ma and gyn/woma as either "attractions to one gender," or "attractions to multiple genders." It's tricky because this categorization depends on how wide the scope of an individual's attractions are. For example, if someone is ma/androsexual and only attracted to men, they would probably consider themselves monosexual. However, if they are ma/androsexual and simply attracted to masculinity, this could put them under the multisexual umbrella, seeing as they could be drawn to masculine men, masculine women, masculine non-binary people, or anyone masculine. In the end, it all depends on which category (if any) the person who claims the labels feels they belong in.[153]

Same gender loving/SGL: This identity refers to **Black LGBTQIA+ individuals.** This identity was created in the 1990s in an effort to engage and affirm black culture, history, and existence in the LGBTGIA+ community.

Below Marquis explains why he describes himself as "same gender loving."[154]

While I generally identify as a gay man, I appreciate the umbrella term of "same-gender loving." Too often, we tend to focus the narratives of the entire community on gay people, not considering those who aren't gay (eg. bi, pan, ace, etc. people). This is where I prefer the umbrella terms like queer and SGL. They're more inclusive. I also know there are people who take on the SGL descriptor because the term "gay" comes with a history of marginalizing more vulnerable identities. Therefore, they find more comfort in SGL, which I totally get.

For me, being same gender loving is an interesting and complex experience. I can't look at my homosexuality in a vacuum. I also have to consider how that identity intersects with my being a Black cis male. The conventional belief is that we have to wear multiple hats at once,

153. You will find that a repeating motif in this book is that many of these identities are precariously complex. Defining and organizing them is challenging as there is no "one right way" to do so.
154. Find more Marquis here: http://bit.ly/2cGs4o7

but I believe it's more so wearing one distinct and unique hat. I'm very much an advocate of Black liberation and empowerment, but I also have to ensure my identity as a same-gender loving person is respected and considered in the process.

This complicates how I navigate queer/LGBTQIA+ spaces because the narratives and experiences most prevalently held up in those spaces, are heavily centered on white, cis people (men, specifically). That's what's considered the "default". So in addition to ensuring my autonomy as a gay man is respected and ensured in Black spaces, I have to do the same in same-gender loving spaces (which often isn't the case, unfortunately).

My personal goal is centering the experiences of Black, queer and trans people and that's where I find the most safety, comfort and empowerment.

Pat yourself on the back, because by this point you've absorbed a massive amount of information. 80 different identities to be exact! I know it might feel like an overwhelming information overload, so let's allow ourselves a short break from all this learning and do some reflecting.

Let's take what we've covered so far and apply it to some self-analysis. Ask yourself, have any words surprised you thus far? Have you discovered any words you might want to try on? Were there any words you know for certain just aren't for you? If you're still in the process of figuring yourself out, I encourage you to pick up a pen and answer the following questions:

- Do your sexual and romantic attractions totally match?

- Which gender(s) do you find attractive (if any)?

- How strongly do you experience attractions?

- How often/intensely do your attractions change?

- Are you currently questioning anything about your identity?

- Are there words we've covered that you think might fit your orientations?

CONCLUSION

Truth be told, I am afraid to write this conclusion. I am afraid because the conclusion signifies the end of this book's story collection, writing, research, rewriting, editing, rewriting, fact checking, and more rewriting. It's 11:42pm on August 28th, 2016, I'm about to turn in a final draft to my editor, and that terrifies me. The text is currently far from perfect, but what I need to do is breathe, and accept that it simply never will be. Our language and understanding of sexual and gender identities is changing too constantly and too rapidly for a project like this to ever completely "get it right."

This really isn't the worst problem to have though. In fact, it's pretty awesome! It means people are continuously creating new words to validate and acknowledge others. Once these identity words are created, the language associated with them and used to explain them is repeatedly being altered and adjusted to keep said terms inclusive and comfy. We should celebrate this! While learning about gender and sexual diversity may be a never-ending adventure, we are making progress, and that is exciting.

One of my fantastic editors, Kristin Russo, read this conclusion and then challenged me to answer this question: if things are always changing, why write a book? I imagine many readers might be asking the same thing, and I think addressing this is important. Yes. Perhaps in a few years this book will become outdated or irrelevant. However, if this text provides any useful education or offers someone's identity some much needed validation at any point, then all the work has become worth it to me.

It's also my hope that this book inspires discussion. Maybe someone will disagree with how I chose to explain a term and seek out a better way. This might lead to a deeper analysis and discourse of the term which results in an even better, more inclusive definition. I'm happy for this book to be just a stepping stone for an identity's final explanation.

Finally, now that you have digested this massive amount of information, let's talk about what you are expected to do with it. The short answer is, your best. I remember when I heard many of these terms for the first time. While I wish I could say each word was easy for me to understand, remember, and implement in my everyday language, that would be a flat out lie. I've had countless moments of overwhelming confusion in my learning. Sometimes it takes weeks, months, even years for me to totally grasp the meaning of some of these labels and concepts.

If this is how you currently feel (overwhelmed, confused, and scared you might forget something or make a mistake), or have ever felt, that is understandable. No reasonable person is expecting you to hear these terms and immediately become a perfectly enlightened, flawless ally or LGBTQIA+ community member. In fact, it is inevitable that you *will* make a few mistakes. What is important though, is that you learn from your slip-ups, apologize when they happen, and continue to actively work on listening and educating yourself. That is all anyone can fairly ask of you.

With that, I'd like to say thank you so much for taking the time to read this book and expand your perspective. I'm finding it difficult figuring out how to end this, so to bid you all farewell, I suppose I'll just do what I usually do at the end of my Youtube videos...

Special thanks to these smart people who helped look over and provide feedback on specific sections of the book:

- Lindsey Doe from https://www.youtube.com/user/sexplanations

- Ashley Wylde https://www.youtube.com/user/AshleysWyldeLife

- Moti Lieberman from https://www.youtube.com/user/thelingspace

- Josh from https://www.youtube.com/c/themadhouseofficial

- Douglas from https://twitter.com/book13worm

- Emily Miller, my best friend from my real life.

Special thanks to all the donors who helped make this project possible! Here are those who spent $5 to get their name in the back of this book:

Troy Renoll
Maggie McCormick
Bryony Mason
Anna Mesirca
EricLacerna
Sofia Öhrström
Shira Silkoff
Amber Coulson-Dos Santos
Aiden Orzech
Jessi Parrott
Brook Tylka
Max Matthiesen
Kelly Boler
Joi Isak
Kelly Ceccato
Rhyan Farmer
Micky Lessly
Haylee Irwin
Lydia Krantz
Axelle MICHEL
Al Howard

Dennis Krause
Juliana Castaneda
Valentina López González
Katie Walker
Alyssa Zajac
Megan Carroll
Xavier Tilley
Natasha Graver
Winston Lindström
S Fitz
Morgan Williamson
Natasha Davidson
Megan Lundy
Emma Overmaat
Rachel Burns
Jacklyn Kelleher
Meike Faber
Casey-Jean Brown
Stacie Irving
Léa Khoury
Zayda Fleming

Cara Closs
Mira Kailanko
Lydia Hill
Madalyn Hardwick
Flávia Salles
Emma Nielsen
Bente Verhulst
Ella McFarlane
Aidan McCusker
Matt Heneghan
Kay M
Frida Lust
Finn Sofroniou
Pauline Julien
Emily Rapp
Saana Herranen
Margarita Gaydarova
Bloo Freeman
Rachel Lea
Len, Kaito and Luka Love!
Ciara-Jane Sheridan
Rachel Bard
Danielle Whitfield
Michelle Peters
Rae Nooney
Khaliyah Carter
Michael Pantis
Eric Svensson
Elsa Erenmalm
Kelly Virtucio
Nicole De Laet
Isabella Darrigan
John Maloney
Amy Löwenadler
Dewi Metzger
Julie Dahlhus
Lavender Truth
Zoe Dinnean
Miishen Willis
Nicole Campos
Jae Millard
Alice Wathen
Florentin Bieder
Darcey Gardner
Dominic Hayes

Jasmine Parsons
Katie Gribble
Logan Dwyer
Erin Douglas
Rowen Arntzberg
Clare Harbin
Samuel J Day
Charlotte Anstett
Margot Spencer
Avery Runge
Maki Montminy
Mikayla Corrigan
Felix Böhner
Anja Lampesberger
Benjamin Ward
Campbell Trotter
Jeanni Floyd
Rhiannon Barber
Aude Bunisset
Sonja van Scheijen
Sadie Heartman
Nora Goerne
Layna Gardiner
Cory Calvert
Noelle Lampe
Niamh McCarthy
Alma Karlsson
Lulu Gettel
Caitlin Corbett
Iwan Evans
Sophie Jeffries
Maddy Marshall
Heather Bower Lee
Matthew Reynolds
Kim-Lan Vo
Shauna Longshore
David Phillips
Zophie Stiles
Jill Deklotz
Andrea Casas
Grace Garas
Cati Davies
Sophia Bisignano-Vadino
Daniela Hilzendegen
Derek Moore

Charmaine Morrison-Mills
Sarah Estelle Barrow
Dana Winter
Grace Watson
itsKaity Cat
Russ Blake
Jenifer Gamelli
Lindsey Johnson
Rachel Trusewicz
Sarah Williams
Sid Achenbach
Elyse Peterson
Sarah Gitlin
Natalie Valett
Caitlin Giron
Lo Johansson
Jeanni Floyd
shane walsh
Phoebe Holder
Maia R
Kerry McDermott
Amy Kerr
Ashley Anderson
Sarah Parker
Savannah Verner
Eddie Allen
Kailin Cluff
Genevieve Henderson
William Dipert
Bryanna Hesse
Jen Hurd
Eloise May
Alex Colburn
Kaitlyn Fagan
Pat Shafer
Natasha Fincher
Brandon Ling
Ro Fell
Claudia A
Stephen DeLay
Sydney Nelson
Brian Morgan
anastasia zacharia
nancy le
Vanessa Noel

Sabrina Oney
Elliot Miles
Ivy Ride
Liam Blombquist
Christine Vandermark
Shannon Humphrey
Morgan Pearce
N. Lily McCarthy
Nelly Rubio
Taylor Danger
Sam Beatty
Danny Bettencourt
Laney Portelance
Olivia Koch
Lizzy Seitz
Noah Wisham
Bonnie Newton
Natalie Richardson
Giovanni Bisanti
Elaine Chau
Jennifer Morris
David Barelli
Moira Clunie
Katie Farris
Coen Flemming
Regina Leslie
Sára Bícová
Dominika &Laura
Laura Rawlings
Alexander Vessel
Robbie Hess
Hope Anastasia
Sarah Dell
William Dipert
Jessica Wicks
Tess Clothier
Elizabeth Leduc
Selene Meza
Ina Hristova
Brittany Waldean
Ruth Campion
Siri LA
Riley Mullen
Karen Roop
Emily Brown

Marte Vestly
Svenja Linberg
Emma Nordanger
Anna Hayes
Sebastian Hitzelburger
Georgia Peacock
Eleanor Hollindrake
Nanna Wilk-Zerahn
Charlotte Jordan
Gwen Kaufmann
Tressalynn Owens
Amanda Randall
Taylor Hendricks
Raven Yankee
Sara Mortensen
Christi Kerr
Kelsey VanSuch
Cara Nordengren
Alexis Porter
Megan Lee
Abbie Richter
Casey Herger
Chey Knippelberg
Kerri LaMarche
Frey Workman
Brooke N
Lane Lamb
Samantha Darr
Ivanna Ajakpo
Lilac Blau
Shannon Crutchfield
Georgia Purkiss
Sinead Hook
Anette Wyroda
Lorelei Watson
Chiara Pietrini
Karina Pil
Kristina Tomaszewski
Reed Chapman
Anya Walton
Alicia Cheale
Justine Lorenz
Daniel Orr
Clé Reymond
Isaac Davis

Serenity Berry
Brianna Watson
Caterina Borracci
Kristopher Snedeker
Janel Gist
Katie Vaughan
Jessica Lynn L.
Emily Rogers
Taylor Hays
Destiny Davis
Rylee Davis
Marie Arnold
Lorien Waymire
Mia Xantidis
Arin Yardley
Adrienne Gauthier
Gabriella Rincón
Eilidh Gow
Nancy Ross
Deyonna Dinius
Dadisi Trower
Tania Stephansen
Jennifer Kostenius
Bethany Francey
Lucy Philips-Roberts
Luke Homer
Phoebe C.
Harpy Bruder
Sharna Patten-Walker
Laura Summersall
Nate Burrows
Catriona Poh
Michelle Meek
Amie Benson
Amy Li
Bryan Jones
Janel Vallejo
Katie Sorensen
Caroline Dignard
DeAnna LePree
Mikaela & Mary Malina
Eric Metzloff
Bethany Radloff
Christian Budhi
Kristina Foley

Annabella Campbell
Giorgiana Spinu
Costin Rosca
Rachel T
Noa YakobShvili
Mic Kupis
Maja Lecher
Charlène Marceau
Jesse Lindenberg
Bella Holt-Piper
Samantha Dudics
Kelly O'Brien
Marion Debock
Naomi Ruys
Purity Galvan
Autumn Osburn
Daphne Titus-Glover
Tilly England
Kayla Sawyer
India Sterling-Fidler
Oliver Suarez
Emily Ludwig
Kelsie Adelaide Schulz
Zoe Lyons
Maren Barnes
Priscila Tchorbadjian
Melody Estorga
Jes Koros
Hannah MacDonald

Mariel McKinney
Doe Mori
Laia Reed
Alex Nickel
Meghan Gallagher
Jerimiah Robey
Fret Highway (Amos Garren)
Matthew Dever
Riley Sanford
Ashley Jensen
Melanie Polo
Kira Copp
Jillian Salmon
Rebecca Dizon
Amanda Curr
Kelsey Tucker
Giulia Curcelli
Daniela Mackin
Amanda Wright
Erin Roach
Paisley Trent
Amber Kober
Hailey Rode
Leslie A. Sanchez
Chloe Rode
Leah Robinson-Gadea
Antonella Demurtas
Kristen Lozo

Terms I might unpack in future books:

Pomosexual

Trans*

Constellation

Polyamory

Monogamish

Plantonic attraction

Aesthetic attraction

Alterous Attraction

Sensual Attraction

Squish

Zucchini

QPR/queer platonic relationship

Non-Monogamy

Cupiosexual/rmantic

"No Romo"

Amatonormativity

Libido

Ace of Hearts, Spades, Clubs, Diamonds

Sex Positivity

Stone

Paper

Paper Mache

Autochoriasexual

Akoisexual/romantic

Sapphic

Achillean

"Of center"

Enbian

More nifty reads:

Trans Bodies, Trans Selves: A Resource for the Transgender Community by Laura Erickson-Schroth

Whipping Girl by Julia Serano

Excluded: Making Feminist and Queer Movements More Inclusive by Julia Serano

The Gender Book by Mel Reiff and Jay Mays

This Is a Book for Parents of Gay Kids: A Question & Answer Guide to Everyday Life by Dannielle Owens-Reid Kristin Russo

Gender Outlaws: The Next Generation by Kate Bornstein and S. Bear Bergman

Transgender 101: A Simple Guide to a Complex Issue by Nicholas M Teich

Anything that loves by Charles "Zan" Christensen and Carol Queen PhD

Fun Home by Alison Bechdel

Tomboy by Liz Prince

PoMoSexuals: Challenging Assumptions About Gender and Sexuality by Carol Queen and Lawrence Schimel

The Invisible Orientation: An Introduction to Asexuality by Julie Sondra Decker

Ace & Proud: An Asexual Anthology by A.K. Andrews

Sex or Ice cream?: Secrets of an Asexual; Asexuality in a Sexed Up World-A Thought-Provoking and Comically Quirky Memoir by Ana Navarro

Lumberjanes by Noelle Stevenson and Shannon Watters

Queer Theory, Gender Theory by Riki Wilchins

My New Gender Workbook: A Step-by-Step Guide to Achieving World Peace Through Gender Anarchy and Sex Positivity by Kate Bornstein

Queer Theory: An Introduction by Annamarie Jagose

Gender Failure Ivan Coyote and Rae Spoon

Gender born Gender made for parents of young TGNC kids

Asexuality: A Breif Introduction by Asexual Archives

The Letter Q by Sarah Moon and James Lecesne

Gender Trouble: Feminism and the Subversion of Identity by Judith Butler

Terms and identity index!